Comprehension, Interpretation and Criticism

In three stages leading to 5th year examinations

G. R. HALSON, M.A.

SENIOR ENGLISH MASTER RUGELEY GRAMMAR SCHOOL

STAGE 3

LONGMAN

LONGMAN GROUP LIMITED
London

*Associated companies, branches and representatives
throughout the world*

First published 1963
Ninth impression 1974

ISBN 0 582 21641 9

*Printed in Hong Kong by
Sheck Wah Tong Printing Press*

Contents

Acknowledgments

We are grateful to the following for permission to include copyright material:
The author for an extract from *Tiger in the Smoke* by Margery Allingham; The Bodley Head Ltd. for an extract from *Magnolia Buildings* by Elizabeth Stucley; Chatto & Windus Ltd. for an extract from *The Uses of Literacy* by Richard Hoggart; William Collins, Sons & Co. Ltd. for an extract from *Harvest of Journeys* by Hammond Innes; J. M. Dent & Sons Ltd. for an extract from *Quite Early One Morning* by Dylan Thomas; *The Guardian* for an extract from the article *The Night Riders* by Martin Page, which appeared in the issue of 11 March 1961; Hamish Hamilton Ltd. for an extract from *The Big Sleep* by Raymond Chandler; Hamish Hamilton Ltd. and Zane Grey Inc. for an extract from *Tappan's Burro* by Zane Grey; The Hogarth Press Ltd. for an extract from "The Witnesses" from *Fireman Flower* by William Sansom; Michael Joseph Ltd. for an extract from *There Is a Happy Land* by Keith Waterhouse; the author's agents for an extract from *Selected Essays* by D. H. Lawrence; Lutterworth Press for an extract from *Zoo Quest in Paraguay* by David Attenborough; Penguin Books Ltd. for an extract from *Scowle and Other Papers* by Bernard Hollowood; the author for an extract from *English Journey* by J. B. Priestley; Martin Secker & Warburg Ltd. for an extract from *Weekend in Dinlock* by Clancy Sigal; the author for an extract from "Noah's Ark" from *The Loneliness of the Long Distance Runner* by Alan Sillitoe; the *Sunday Telegraph* for an extract from the article *Steam's Last Mileposts* by Ian Waller, which appeared in the issue of 10 September 1961, and the author for an extract from *Cats* by Brian Vesey-Fitzgerald.

Preface

by J. G. WELCH, B.A.
Head of the Upper School, Tulse Hill School.

Too often in the past comprehension books have set out to test rather than to teach, and some of us in the schools have long been doubtful even about their validity as testing instruments.

There is a growing tendency among progressive teachers of English to make four demands of the good comprehension book:

1 that the extracts are sufficiently long and interesting to "involve" the reader, and of sufficient intrinsic merit to justify their inclusion;
2 that the questions really stimulate close reading and require thoughtful answers rather than the facile lifting of chunks from the text;
3 that vocabulary questions should not measure already acquired definitions, but encourage the "natural" development of word-mastery, that is, by intelligent guessing and deduction from the larger context;
4 that some guidance is given to the development of literary appreciation, with pointers to the study of *how* authors gain their effects.

In satisfying these rigorous demands Mr. Halson has also provided a valuable prose anthology. At all stages his book will require the close co-operation of teacher and pupil, for it is emphatically a book for teachers and not for testers.

Introduction

This book has been designed to appeal to and to cater for the needs of upper forms in Secondary Schools. It is intended as a means of combining the literary and the functional aspects of comprehension.

The functional value of the comprehension exercise is undoubted; it develops the faculties of intelligent, perceptive reading, accurate selection, deduction and explanation, and clear expression – both oral and written. This value is recognised in the vital role played by the comprehension section of the G.C.E. " O " Level English Language Papers and an increasing number of external examination papers, both national and regional. At the same time, in the classroom at any rate, Comprehension should have a more than functional value. It must be closely allied to literary appreciation. The passages used must be virtually a challenging window-display of wares worth acquiring. The questions must, to carry the analogy further, be the sales-talk to encourage the student to acquire and enjoy these wares, not to remove his desire to buy.

Bearing these intentions in mind, great care has been taken with the selection of the passages. They have been chosen, initially, with the idea of appealing to the reader, so that they can be read, in the first instance, purely for general enjoyment without reference to the questions. From this point of view the book can be regarded to some extent as an anthology of contemporary or near-contemporary prose. As far as possible the passages cover either a complete description or episode, or they are taken to a suitable point of climax in the hope either that the student will be encouraged to acquire and read the book for himself or that the teacher may consider it worth while to continue reading the book to the class. In consequence, the length of passages varies considerably, but it has been felt that from the point of view of literary appreciation as well as that of a full comprehension of the aims of a writer, longer passages must be admitted rather than curtailed merely in order to produce a standard length. In choosing the passages, their stylistic merits, similarly, do not conform to a set literary standard. The main consideration has been whether the passage is of a good standard with regard to its specialised intentions. Accordingly, it is felt that, with these reservations, there is every justification for introducing passages from outstanding thriller writers such as Margery Allingham and Raymond Chandler, journalists writing for national newspapers and magazines, travellers presenting accounts of their experiences, and novelists presenting their characters from an intensely regional and realistic point of view. It follows that these passages can, to some extent, be grouped for the purpose of a closer comparative study of styles of writing and their relation to the social aspects of contemporary literature. Some suggestions for this type of use of the passages appear frequently in Section C of the exercises.

The exercises are designed to work towards a fuller appreciation and understanding of the particular passage rather than towards an acquiring of the techniques peculiar to any one external examination. Thus, no rigid number of questions has been adopted, either in each exercise, or in each section of the exercises. The number depends entirely on the problems presented by the individual passage. On the other hand, the general style of the questions should prove of value in preparing students in the broad techniques involved in comprehension exercises set in external examinations.

The exercises are divided into three sections. Section A mostly involves the careful selection and restatement of details given in the passage and the deduction of conclusions implicit in the details given. Section B is more concerned with stylistic implications and particularly with the meanings and implications of specific words and phrases. Here, the tendency to ask for bald definitions of words taken out of their context has been avoided; instead, the words or phrases to be explained have been re-quoted within their context so that vocabulary study remains an integral part of the process of comprehension instead of a section viewed in cold isolation. In Section B too, reference is made to simile, metaphor and other devices such as paradox and climax where the understanding of such devices is an important part of the full appreciation of the passage and its literary merits. Section C is not intended, initially, at any rate, as a written exercise. It has been included purposely to stimulate comment and further discussion and it has been designed to suggest possible bases for discussion and even research, stimulated by the teacher. Whereas Sections A and B are related solely to the internal comprehension of the passage, Section C is an attempt to encourage studies both of the wider implications of the work or the style of a writer and of the similarities between writers either in connection with their regional interests or in connection with their specialist fields of writing.

The book contains 18 passages, broadly graded in terms of length and for relative difficulty. It thus provides material for regular comprehension, but, since the passages do not form part of a continuous course, they can be used selectively by the teacher or perhaps in series which will stimulate study of a particular type of writing.

Finally, it is hoped that although the exercises will give plenty of scope for written work, they will also receive plenty of oral consideration. The importance of the teacher, both as guide and interpreter, and the importance of oral as well as written comprehension studies, cannot be overstressed if Comprehension is to achieve its full value and not remain a mere academic exercise.

The Notes on Authors, which will be found at the end of the book, are designed further to introduce the pupil to the authors of these extracts, and to encourage them to explore their other writings.

1 Making Geography Live

Really, Charteris is too bad. The Staff Room is seething with discontent. Although Charteris has more or less been sent to Coventry he persists in his efforts to teach geography realistically or, as he so often proclaims, "to make geography live". This week, for instance, he is "doing" North Africa – he has been "doing" it since last August. He has converted his room into a sandpit in an attempt to reproduce the Libyan campaign in miniature. Naturally the sand does not remain in his room. It is mostly in my French readers, in my ink-wells and
10 in the pencil sharpener (sabotage).

On Wednesday afternoon (as on so many Wednesday afternoons) I was waiting to teach Lower Threes the rudiments of the verb *faire* causatively. They were already five minutes late when Migson Minimus burst in to say "Mr. Charteris's apologies, Sir, and would you mind if we're two minutes late as we're shelling Benghazi?" – and to depart on the instant. Soon afterwards the whole school was made forcibly aware of the heavy barrage that our fellows were putting up to cover an infantry advance on Benina aerodrome. There were loud
20 reports from pop-guns and paper bags, and a continuous bedlam which I presume was meant to represent the sound of shells passing overhead. The whole school stopped work. It had to. At long last cheers broke out, the Union Jack was hoisted over the Government Buildings, the door opened and Lower Three and a lot more sand came pouring out. I said nothing to Charteris on that occasion.

I had given him a piece of my mind only the previous week after the fiasco of the French exam. You see, not content with covering the floors of the school with the clay mountains of
30 Abyssinia, the sands of Libya and the snows of Norway, he has the effrontery to decorate the walls of every room with hideous maps and posters. In my French room he went to the extreme limit of impertinence in pasting a gaudy futuristic travel poster

of St. Moritz over a notice which I had carefully drawn in Indian ink to emphasise the importance of such points as "After 'after' use compound infinitive," "me, te, se, nous, vous, . . . etc.," and "Pronoun object goes before the verb except in the imperative affirmative".

40 Question 5 of my French Examination Paper for Remove A read "Write an essay of 200 words on Paris". When I marked the answers I was astounded to find that without exception they began – "Paris est situe sur les deux rives de la Seine, à une altitude variant de 26 m. a 218 m. . . ." and continued for 200 words in each case exactly the same. Of course, I realised what had happened. The boys had copied unashamedly from one of Charteris's tom-fool P.L.M. posters revealing the glories of France. He had ruined my exam and I told him so in no uncertain terms.

Perhaps his worst fault is in connection with the Staff Room 50 newspapers. As soon as Bagsworthy, the old porter, places them on the racks (at 8.20 a.m.) Charteris bounds up from his chair brandishing a pair of editorial scissors and calmly relieves every newspaper of its maps. These he distributes to the group captains of his geography-room campaigns. Quite naturally we resent this mutilation of our reading matter. A few weeks ago I lost sixpence in a small bet with Cartwright, the chemistry man, who held the view that Hong Kong is insular. My own opinion that it was peninsular was directly traceable to Charteris's misdemeanours with the newspapers.

60 Still, if I have anything to complain of, poor Wilkinsummer has more. Wilkinsummer tends the school garden, which was last year growing excellent crops of potatoes, spinach and onions. I forgot to mention that for his major attempts to make geography live, Charteris has utilised the playing fields. Across the Second XI cricket-pitch there now runs a stream loaded with silt which it deposits beneath the goalposts on the hockey-pitch. Nailed to the cross-bar runs a notice in the neat calligraphy of Charteris: "Alluvial fan-delta conditions." However, I began with Wilkinsummer. Charteris and his play-70 mates dug realistic trenches and constructed earthworks to illustrate a lesson on "The Geography behind the Fall of

2

France ". These trenches and earthworks ran alongside Wilkin-summer's cabbage patch. Imagine his horror when one day he sees Monitor Whigmore's head pop up in the middle of his onion bed and (the next moment) watches the greater part of his garden disappear into a maze of human warrens. Charteris, in apology, merely said " Perhaps we did sap a little too far ".

Charteris plans to " do " the Russian campaign shortly. In that case he will almost certainly turn off the school hot-water system, and I shall hand in my notice to the Governors.

80

BERNARD HOLLOWOOD
Scowle and Other Papers

A. Comprehension and Deduction

1 From the evidence of the opening sentences what is the imaginary occupation of the writer of this article?

2 Explain, briefly and in your own words, Charteris's methods of teaching geography.

3 Why would these methods be unpopular with the staff of most schools?

4 Why would these methods be popular with the children, perhaps?

5 Sum up all the ways in which the lessons on the Libyan desert war affected the routine of the school.

6 Explain, in your own words, the various annoyances caused to the writer by the geography teacher's studies of France.

7 What part do the staff-room newspapers play in the scheme of geography lessons?

8 Explain, in your own words, how this part again caused annoyance to the writer.

9 Why were the school playing fields of great value to Charteris in his geography lessons?

10 Explain how this use came to affect the school garden.

3

B. *Interpretation and Criticism*

1 What does the opening sentence of this account reveal of the writer's state of mind and feelings?

2 What does the statement "Charteris has more or less been sent to Coventry" mean? (lines 2-3)

3 "He persists in his efforts to teach geography realistically or, as he so often proclaims, 'to make geography live'." (lines 3-4)

(i) What does the use of the word "proclaims" instead of a simple word such as "says" tell us of Charteris's character and manner of speaking?

(ii) What does its use and the general tone of the remarks in this paragraph tell us of the writer's opinions of and feelings towards Charteris?

4 (*a*) Who do you think were "our fellows"? (line 18)

(*b*) What further proof have you in paragraph 2 of the answer you have just given?

5 The writer refers to "a gaudy futuristic travel poster". (line 33) Give some details of the type of poster which you think would fit this description.

6 Why does the writer use the word "editorial" to describe the scissors referred to in line 52?

7 Which statement in paragraph 5 suggests that Charteris organises his geography on military lines?

8 What is the difference between the words "insular" and "peninsular"? (lines 57 and 58)

9 "A maze of human warrens." (line 76) What does this phrase mean as used here? With what do we usually associate the word "warrens" and why is the association apt here?

10 "Perhaps we did sap a little too far." (line 77) By considering why certain soldiers in the Royal Engineers are called sappers, and by looking carefully at the context of this remark try to explain the meaning of the word "sap" as used here.

C. Comment and Discussion

1   Much of the humour of this passage stems from the fact that the writer is deliberately making fun of Charteris's teaching methods. How is this done?

2   As in many humorous passages, exaggeration is present. At what points do you consider that the author is deliberately exaggerating?

3   Some of the humour is sheer situation comedy depending purely on events to provide natural amusement. Pick out some of these situations and consider why they are automatically a source of fun.

4   Much humour also has a serious intention. Here it could be that the writer is making fun of Charteris's *methods* rather than of Charteris the man. Try to discover how the writer suggests this intention. Why does this lack of personal malice make the humour of the passage more acceptable to the reader?

5   For another example of humorous writing see Beasts in the Bathroom (No. 3, page 11).

2 *Shots in the Dark*

He showed about four o'clock. A cream-coloured coupe stopped in front of the store and I caught a glimpse of the fat face and the Charlie Chan moustache as he dodged out of it and into the store. He was hatless and wore a belted green leather rain-coat. I couldn't see his glass eye at that distance. A tall and very good-looking kid in a jerkin came out of the store and rode the coupé off around the corner and came back walking, his glistening black hair plastered with rain.

Another hour went by. It got dark and the rain-clouded
10 lights of the stores were soaked up by the black street. Street-car bells jangled crossly. At around five-fifteen the tall boy in the jerkin came out of Geiger's with an umbrella and went after the cream-coloured coupe. When he had it in front Geiger came out and the tall boy held the umbrella over Geiger's bare head. He folded it, shook it off and handed it into the car. He dashed back into the store. I started my motor.

The coupe went west on the boulevard, which forced me to make a left turn and a lot of enemies, including a motor-man who stuck his head out into the rain to bawl me out. I was two
20 blocks behind the coupé before I got in the groove. I hoped Geiger was on his way home. I caught sight of him two or three times and then made him turning north into Laurel Canyon Drive. Half-way up the grade he turned left and took a curving ribbon of wet concrete which was called Laverne Terrace. It was a narrow street with a high bank on one side and a scattering of cabin-like houses built down the slope on the other side, so that their roofs were not very much above road level. Their front windows were masked by hedges and shrubs. Sodden trees dripped all over the landscape.

30 Geiger had his lights on and I hadn't. I speeded up and passed him on a curve, picked a number off a house as I went by and turned at the end of the block. He had already stopped. His car lights were tilted in at the garage of a small house with

6

a square box hedge so arranged that it masked the front door completely. I watched him come out of the garage with his umbrella up and go in through the hedge. He didn't act as if he expected anybody to be tailing him. Light went on in the house. I drifted down to the next house above it, which seemed empty but had no signs out. I parked, aired out the convert-
40 ible, had a drink from my bottle, and sat. I didn't know what I was waiting for, but something told me to wait. Another army of sluggish minutes dragged by.

Two cars came up the hill and went over the crest. It seemed to be a very quiet street. At a little after six more bright lights bobbed through the driving rain. It was pitch-black by then. A car dragged to a stop in front of Geiger's house. The filaments of its lights glowed dimly and died. The door opened and a woman got out. A small slim woman in a vagabond hat and a transparent raincoat. She went in through the box maze.
50 A bell rang faintly, light through the rain, a closing door, silence.

I reached a flash out of my car pocket and went down-grade and looked at the car. It was a Packard convertible, maroon or dark brown. The left window was down. I felt for the licence holder and poked light at it. The registration read: Carmen Sternwood, 3765 Alta Brea Crescent, West Hollywood. I went back to my car again and sat and sat. The top dripped on my knees and my stomach burned from the whisky. No more cars came up the hill. No lights went on in the house before which
60 I was parked. It seemed like a nice neighbourhood to have bad habits in.

At seven-twenty a single flash of hard white light shot out of Geiger's house like a wave of summer lightning. As the darkness folded back on it and ate it up a thin tinkling scream echoed out and lost itself among the rain-drenched trees. I was out of the car and on my way before the echoes died.

There was no fear in the scream. It had the sound of half-pleasurable shock, an accent of drunkenness, an overtone of pure idiocy. It was a nasty sound. It made me think of men in
70 white and barred windows and hard narrow cots with leather wrist and ankle straps fastened to them. The Geiger hideaway

7

was perfectly silent again when I hit the gap in the hedge and dodged around the angle that masked the front door. There was an iron ring in a lion's mouth for a knocker. I reached for it, I had hold of it. At that exact instant, as if somebody had been waiting for the cue, three shots boomed in the house. There was a sound that might have been a long harsh sigh. Then a soft messy thump. And then rapid footsteps in the house – going away. . . .

RAYMOND CHANDLER
The Big Sleep

A. Comprehension and Deduction

1 Where was the writer waiting, and for what purpose?
2 What evidence is there in paragraph 1 that the writer is well aware of Geiger's appearance and has probably met him before?
3 What duties did the boy in the jerkin perform whilst he was under observation?
4 What were the main difficulties involved in following Geiger?
5 What was the writer's object in overtaking Geiger when he stopped?
6 What suggested to the writer that the house next door to Geiger's might *not* be empty?
7 How did the writer discover the identity of the driver of the car which stopped outside Geiger's?
8 Why did this seem a suitable neighbourhood for crime?
9 What was the writer's reaction when he heard the scream? What worried him about its quality?
10 What prevented him from knocking at the door?

B. Interpretation and Criticism

1 What is the effect of the statement of exact times of various happenings by the writer? To what extent does this add to your enjoyment of the story, and why?

2 (a) Why should street-car bells jangle crossly? (lines 10-11)
   (b) What does the word "jangled" tell you about the type
   of noise they made?

3 What is the meaning of the phrase "bawl me out" in line
   19?

4 Explain the meaning and the aptness of the metaphor
   "ribbon" in the phrase "curving ribbon of wet concrete".
   (line 24)

5 Explain the meaning of the metaphor "masked" in the
   phrase "masked by hedges and shrubs". (line 28) Why do
   the associations of the word make it an effective word to use
   in this particular setting?

6 What are the implications of the word "drifted" in the
   statement "I drifted down to the next house above it", particularly in relation to the manner in which the writer
   drove his car? (line 38)

7 What is the effect of the style of writing on the build-up of
   atmosphere in the sentence, "A bell rang faintly, light
   through the rain, a closing door, silence." What *kind* of
   effect is conveyed? (lines 50-51)

8 What is the reason for and the effect of the repetition of
   the words "and sat"? (line 57)

9 How, in paragraph 7, does the writer convey the idea of
   the intensity of the darkness and the momentary intensity
   of the light? (Answer in detail.)

10 Which comment in the final paragraph reveals the typical
   detective's eye for detail, even in moments of high excitement?

C. Comment and Discussion

1 This is a typical passage from one of American writer
   Raymond Chandler's thrillers. Which features of the description are an automatic source of excitement to the reader
   of thrillers?

2 Chandler is a master of the brief, vivid word picture and
   of the type of understatement which implies a great deal.
   This skilful use of detail is what raises his style above that

of the ordinary thriller writer – this and a very individual sardonic humour. Pick out examples of these aspects of his writing.

3 Select some Americanisms in the style of this passage. Consider to what extent they make the passage more vivid and enjoyable.

4 What are the advantages of writing this type of narrative in the first person?

3 Beasts in the Bathroom

For the animal collector, there is no more useful room than the bathroom. I first discovered this truth on an expedition in Africa, when we stayed in a rest-house the bathroom of which was so primitive that we had little compunction in foregoing its largely hypothetical amenities and using it as an annexe of our embryonic zoo. Its only claim to its title was a monstrous, somewhat chipped enamel bath which stood majestically in the middle of the otherwise bare floor of red earth. It still sported a plug, shackled to the brass overflow by a heavy chain, and its taps were bravely labelled "Hot" and "Cold", but if the water had ever flowed through their tarnished Victorian nozzles, it must have done so in some earlier more distinguished situation, for here they were unconnected to any pipes and the only running water within miles flowed through a nearby river.

But though this bathroom had little to commend it as a place in which to wash, it provided excellent accommodation for animals. A large fluffy owl chick relished the gloom, so similar to the dim light of its nesting hole, and perched happily on a stick thrust through the rush walls across one corner. Six corpulent toads inhabited the dank clammy recesses beneath the deep end of the bath, and later a young crocodile, a yard long, spent several weeks lounging in the bath itself.

To be truthful, the bath was not the ideal home for the crocodile because, although he was unable to scale its smooth sides during the day, at night he seemed to draw on extra sources of energy and each morning we found him wandering loose on the floor. We took it in turns, as one of the regular before-breakfast chores, to drop a wet flannel over his eyes, pick him up by the back of his neck while he was still blindfold, and put him back, grunting with indignation, into his enamel pond.

Since that time, we have kept humming birds and chameleons, pythons, electric eels and otters in bathrooms as far apart

as Surinam, Java and New Guinea, and when Dick Barton showed us the elegantly appointed private one at Ita Caabo, I had noted appreciatively that it was by far the most suitable that we had ever had at our disposal. Its floor was tiled, its walls of concrete, the door stout and close fitting and it was furnished not only with a bath possessing fully functional taps,
40 but a lavatory and hand-basin as well. The possibilities were immense.

When we first flew in the company's plane, I had decided that there would be no room in it for any animals on the return trip to Asuncion, but as the days passed, and the precise memory of the plane's size began to fade, I managed to convince myself that there must surely be enough space on board for just one or two small creatures. It seemed a criminal waste not to take some advantage of the bathroom's potentialities.

I found the first lodger for the bathroom one day when I
50 was out riding on the camp shortly after a heavy rainstorm. The paddocks were waterlogged and in the hollows wide shallow pools had formed. As I rode past one of them, I noticed a small frog-like face peering above the surface of the water, gravely inspecting me. As I dismounted, the face disappeared in a muddy swirl. I tied my horse to the fence and sat down to wait. Soon the face appeared again from the farther edge of the pool. I walked round towards it and was soon close enough to see that whatever else this inquisitive little creature might be, it was not a frog. Again it vanished and swam away
60 beneath the surface, stirring up a cloudy line as it went. The trail stopped as the animal settled on the bottom. I put my hand into the water and brought up a small turtle.

He had a beautifully marked underside, patterned in black and white, and a neck so long that he was unable to retract it straight inwards like a tortoise, but had had to fold it sideways. He was a side-necked turtle – not a rare creature, but an engaging one, and I was quite sure that we could find room in the aeroplane for one so small and attractive, even if he had to travel in my pocket. The bath, half-filled, with a few
70 boulders in the deep end on which he could climb when he was bored with swimming, made him an excellent home.

12

Two days later, in one of the streams, we found him a mate. As the pair of them lay motionless on the bottom of the bath, each displayed two brilliant black and white fleshy tabs which hung down from beneath their chins like lawyers' bands. It may be that these odd appendages, which their owner can move about if it wishes to do so, serve as lures to attract small fish fatally close to the turtle's mouth, as it lies unobtrusive and stone-like on the bottom of the pond. But our turtles had no need to use them for each evening we begged some raw meat, from the kitchen and offered it to them with a pair of forceps. They fed eagerly, shooting their necks forward to engulf the meat in their mouths. As soon as they had finished their meal, we took them out of the water and let them wander around on the tiled floor while we used the bath for its more conventional purpose.

DAVID ATTENBOROUGH
Zoo Quest in Paraguay

A. Comprehension and Deduction

1 How could David Attenborough tell that the room about which he is writing at the beginning of this passage was indeed a bathroom?
2 Why could the room not actually be used as a bathroom?
3 From the information given in paragraph 1, when, approximately, was the room planned as a bathroom?
4 Explain clearly when and why a flannel was an essential part of Attenborough's equipment when using this particular bathroom.
5 From the information given in this passage explain in detail the various uses to which a well equipped bathroom could be put in storing zoo specimens.
6 What was the main reason for Attenborough deciding to take a few specimens back by plane to Asuncion?

7 (a) What was the first specimen which he captured?
   (b) Where exactly was it found?
   (c) How was it caught?
   (d) In what way did the weather conditions at the time aid its discovery?
8 How was this creature made as comfortable as possible in captivity?
9 Explain, in your own words, how, according to Attenborough, these creatures might attract and catch their prey.
10 Why were the two specimens allowed to wander round in the bathroom after their evening meal?

B. Interpretation and Criticism

1 Express simply what the writer means when he says "We had little compunction in foregoing its largely hypothetical amenities." (lines 4-5)
2 How are the words "Its only claim to its title" and the word "majestically" (lines 6 and 7) related metaphorically? (i.e. What do the implied comparisons have in common?) Why do these implied comparisons add to the writer's humorous ridicule here?
3 What are the meanings and implications of the words "tarnished" and "Victorian" as used in describing the nozzles of the taps? (line 11)
4 Which word used in paragraph 2 suggested that the toads found the bathroom healthy and congenial? What is the meaning of this word?
5 What do the words "relished" (line 17) and "lounging" (line 22) tell us about the respective feelings of the chick and the crocodile towards life in the bathroom? Why do the words convey these feelings effectively?
6 What is the meaning of the verb "to scale"? (line 24) Why is this a particularly appropriate verb to use in this context?
7 Explain in your own words the meaning of the phrase "elegantly appointed" when applied to a bathroom. (line 35)

8 Re-express in a simple phrase the phrase "fully-functional taps". (line 39)

9 What was Attenborough implying when he said, referring to the bathroom at Ita Caabo, that "the possibilities were immense"? (lines 40-41)

10 Which single word in paragraph 5 has broadly the same meaning in the passage as "possibilities"? (line 40)

11 Which words, used to describe the turtles in the final paragraph, illustrate how "unobtrusive" they are?

12 What does Attenborough mean when he concludes, "we used the bath for its more conventional purpose"? What had been its unconventional use on this occasion?

C. Comment and Discussion

1 The comic moments in this description are connected with the keeping of animals and reptiles in bathrooms. To what extent does the humour lie in situation comedy pure and simple? See also "Making Geography Live" (No. 1).

2 Give examples of the ways in which David Attenborough's style of writing and choice of words and phrases help to make the account more humorous.

4 *The Nottingham Goose Fair*

Long before the fair itself came into view you saw its great roof
of lighted sky. It had not been allowed to sprawl but was strictly
confined to a large rectangular piece of ground – and within
this area not an inch of room was wasted – the roundabouts
and shows and stalls were laid out in rows and as close together
as possible; the lights and the noise buffeted your senses – you
seemed to walk into a square of blazing bedlam. Its narrow
avenues were so thickly packed with people that you could
only shuffle along, pressed close on every side. In this crushing
10 mass of gaping and sweating humanity were little children,
some of them hardly more than babies, who had long ago
wearied of all these huge glittering toys, who were worn out
by the late hour, the lights, the noise, the crowd, and either
tottered along like tiny somnambulists or yawned and whimpered over their parents' shoulders. The brazen voices of the
showmen, now made more hideous and gargantuan than ever
by the amplifiers and loud speakers, battered our hearing,
which could not pluck words out of these terrifying noises. The
mechanical organs blared in batteries, so closely ranged that
20 the ear could never detect a single tune: all it heard was the
endless grinding symphony. The real patrons of fairs of this
kind are youngsters in their 'teens; and there were thousands
of them pushing and cat-calling and screaming in the crowd:
the boys, their faces grinning and vacant in the whirl of
coloured light, sometimes looking like members of some sub-
human race surging up from the interior of the earth – the
girls, whose thickly powdered faces were little white masks
without lines but daubed with red and black, looked like dolls
out of some infernal toyshop; and the appearance of them all
30 was fascinating and frightening. And this was Goose Fair, and
Merrie England.

I climbed into the tail of a ruby and emerald fish which,
after I had paid it threepence, rushed up and down and round

16

and round, and mixed the whole fair into a spangled porridge. At the other end of my car, in the fish's mouth, were half a dozen adolescents, all jammed together, and at every dip the girls screamed and screamed, like slavering maenads. Now and then, high above the topmost cluster of electric lights, outlining the platform from which the diver would plunge into a
40 tank with a surface of blazing petrol, there came a glimpse of a misty moon, mild and remote as the benediction of some antique priest. I went into a boxing show, where, for the benefit of a roaring crowd, a local middle-weight ("Hit him, Tom," they cried to him) was battering away at one of the showman's pugs, a thick-set negro with a mere remnant of a face but with a golden-brown torso that wore the bloom on it of ripe fruit. The men were not boxing, they were simply hitting one another, through round after round, and every now and then the negro, who knew his job as a showman, would
50 stagger about, clutch at the ropes, and even fall, pretending a last extremity. At the end of the agreed ten rounds he miraculously revived, looked fierce and made threatening gestures – and then the referee, amid an uproar of excited half-wits, announced that they would fight another five rounds later, but in the meantime would come round with the hat. It was not boxing; it was not even genuine fighting – but a nasty and artful mixture of slogging and acting, and an insult to any but an audience of bloodthirsty oafs. Having no opportunity of learning the negro's opinion of life, which would
60 have been of more interest than his boxing, I left the show. Close by there were gigantic hoots and screams of laughter coming from a mysterious square building labelled "Over the Falls". Never had I heard such brassy bellowings. I paid my threepence, and then found myself in a heaving darkness inside. There were two or three corners to be turned, and at every turn the darkness heaved more violently, and one might have been deep in the hold of a thousand-ton ship in an Atlantic gale. It was then that I realised that the giant laughter, which I could still hear, was not coming from me or from the few
70 others in distress in the dark there, but from a machine. Afterwards I heard several of these machines, hooting and bellowing

with satanic mirth. (Probably they are quietly chuckling now, somewhere on the road or at the back of a shed.) When I was finally shot out, on a downward-moving platform, into the gaping crowd, the machine giggled thunderously and then went off into another brazen peal. Even H. G. Wells, in his earlier and wildly imaginative days, never thought of machines that would laugh for us. He can hear them now: not only laughing for us but also, I suspect, laughing at us. I continued my ex-
80 ploration with that laughter still hurting my ears. While circling round in that fish I had caught a glimpse of a show called "The Ghost Train", which excited my curiosity. When I left the fish, this show had disappeared, but now I suddenly came upon it, with a queue of folk waiting to take their seats in the miniature wooden trains. At last I was given a train, which was immediately pushed through some swing doors and went plunging and bumping into the gloom beyond. It was a perilous journey. Green eyes suddenly glared at me; I rushed to collide with skeletons; hangmen's nooses brushed my fore-
90 head in the dark; dreadful screams tore the thick air; the mad little train hurled me straight at an illuminated blank wall that somehow dissolved into dark space again; so that at the end of two or three minutes I felt that I had had a terrific adventure. I should have enjoyed this piece of grim ingenuity much better if while I was waiting I had not seen two tired little children taken into one of these trains by their idiotic parents, who might have guessed that behind those swing doors there was material enough for a hundred nightmares. It is not as if the children were clamouring for these mysteries. The
100 hour had long past when small children clamoured for anything but home and a bed. It is not always fun being a child in Nottingham during Goose Fair.

J. B. PRIESTLEY
English Journey

A. *Comprehension and Deduction*

1 What are the main features of the general layout of the fair?

2 (*a*) What was Priestley's reaction to seeing little children at the fair?
(*b*) How does he convey this reaction in the passage?

3 Why did the showmen use amplifiers and loudspeakers?

4 (*a*) Who were the main supporters of the fair?
(*b*) Why is this so, do you think?

5 Explain in your own words how Priestley first sampled the fun of the fair.

6 Why did Priestley disapprove of the boxing show?

7 Explain the part played by the negro in this boxing show.

8 (*a*) What did Priestley disapprove of most in his sampling of "Over the Falls"?
(*b*) Why did he disapprove?

9 Although Priestley quite enjoyed his own experience of The Ghost Train, he was worried by one aspect of it. What was this?

10 Try to sum up the reasons for Priestley's critical view of the fair.

B. *Interpretation and Criticism*

1 (*a*) What is the meaning of the word "bedlam" as used here in the phrase "a square of blazing bedlam"? (line 7)
(*b*) Try to discover the origin of the word.

2 What is the meaning and what are the implications of the word "buffeted" in the statement "the noise *buffeted* your senses"? (line 6)

3 Look up the meaning of the word "somnambulist". What therefore, is the critical implication of the simile in the comment, "little children . . . tottered along like tiny somnambulists"? (line 14)

4 What is the meaning of the word "brazen" (line 15) as it is used to describe the voices of the showmen, and why is it aptly used here?

5 "The mechanical organs blared in *batteries,* so closely *ranged* that the ear could never detect a single tune." (lines 19-20) What are the military associations of the two words – "batteries" and "ranged"? What is Priestley therefore implying about the music and the noise?

6 What is the critical implication of the word "daubed" in describing the young girls' make-up? (line 28)

7 (*a*) Why does Priestley admit that the negro "knew his job as a showman"? (line 49)
(*b*) What is the meaning of the word "pug" (line 45) as used here to describe the negro?

8 What is the difference between "slogging" and "punching"? Why does Priestley use the words "slogging" (line 57) and "battering" (line 44) to describe this particular fight?

9 Why does Priestley describe the darkness as "heaving" (line 64) when he visits the attraction "Over the Falls"?

10 Why, do you think, does Priestley suggest that these machines might well be laughing "at us" as well as "for us"?

11 Explain the meaning of Priestley's statement in the final paragraph – "there was material enough for a hundred nightmares". (line 98)

12 Why is the final comment, "It is not always fun being a child in Nottingham during Goose Fair" far more effective in its critical implications than a long tirade on the subject?

C. Comment and Discussion

Much of Priestley's *English Journey* is a grim record of a tour mainly through industrial England during the terrible period of unemployment in the 1930s. Its pungent style and uncompromising descriptions of scenes of poverty make it a most moving social document comparable with similar indictments of 19th-century industrial England made by Charles Dickens. Occasionally in this book the sombre quality of the material is lightened by passages such as this in which a specific scene is brought vividly to life.

1 Consider now those aspects of Priestley's style and vocabulary which bring to life this bustling, seething scene. Try to find examples of slightly exaggerated description which creates the larger-than-life effect of a caricature – e.g. "gigantic hoots", "a square of blazing bedlam". Note his use of evocative verbs (tottered, buffeted, etc.) and adjectives (grinding, brassy, etc.)

2 At the same time consider how his style contrives to remain down-to-earth ("I felt that I had had a terrific adventure") so that one feels that one is being given a personally conducted tour. How much of one's enjoyment of this passage is created by the fact that Priestley's description is concerned with personal impressions rather than the desire to present an impartial picture of the Fair?

3 For another view of The Goose Fair see Going To The Fair (No. 8, page 38).

5 Fire in a Coffee Warehouse

Imagine a patch of marshland in the mist. The blackish earth smokes out its white vapour, there are little mounds where the mist appears to gather in greater density, there are pockets and sloping hollows that sometimes emerge clearly – providing suddenly an ephemeral vista of some few yards – and then as quickly disappear as the white wet fog seeps and drifts all about them. Sometimes the fog hangs immobile, like a terrible pale blindness, and sometimes it wreathes and eddies. Then it has the motion of some slow-moving monster, a caterpillar, waving its head vaguely in search of the food it will so inevitably, so casually swallow.

But in this case the marsh has no surface of black peat – it is a waste land of bad-smelling coffee beans. Coffee beans have poured from their burst sacks and now lie silted in thick mounds for hundreds of feet around. They have been burning, for there has been a fire, and the warehouse that once enclosed them has collapsed many hours ago. So that a few bricks and strange promontories of broken masonry emerge at intervals from the brown swamp of steaming beans. Firemen have quenched the first fury of the fire, but there are still moments of danger ahead. For within the brownish-purple mounds and dunes there still lie muffled nests of fire, deep and unpredictable, smouldering fiercely, corroding upwards as their hidden heat germinates, multiplying themselves in an effort to erupt a combustive exit. Upon these dangerous mounds firemen still pour a ceaseless stream of water. As the water drenches down, a mist of steam rises and, mixing with the smoke, fogs the air thickly.

Above this swamp a fireman seems to float in mid-mist. If you had stood below and looked up, you would have thought he was actually riding the steam, really straddling with the grip of his oilskinned knees the white cloud itself.

But this is the illusion of steam and smoke, for he really

sits astride a broken wall obscured by the white veil of mist. As the mist drifts, you may see a part of the wall. It is some twenty feet high, so that the fireman sits on a precarious seat: he directs the jet from his hose downwards on to the beans, circling here and there as the smoke guides him towards patches of internal fire. The hose is heavy, the water pressure
40 as much as he can hold. So that if something were to slip, the fireman would certainly be thrown off the wall and down into the terrible boiling beans: or he might break his head against some angular rock of masonry. Thus he is careful to keep the ridge of wall gripped between his legs.

We watched those thick-booted legs of his as he leaned forward. We knew well that he forced his body forward because the hose and its live recoil constantly dragged him back. He leant forward. in a sense resting on the firm hose, yet while he rested he had to push as well, for his weight alone could not
50 control that pressure. The insides of his knees were aching as they bruised themselves slowly against the hard brick. Although he was scarcely able to move the position of his body on that constricted wall – occasionally he had to ease his pressed flesh and tired muscles: for the strain of two or three hours in such a cramped position is tremendous. It calls for no quick exertion, no leaps of prowess, but it is like carrying a heavy trunk, when your muscles accumulate their torture with the strain of each added minute, when hard corners bite into your flesh, when out of breath you drop the trunk heavily on a landing,
60 determined to stretch and rest your cramped body before continuing up the next flight of stairs. But high up on the wall you cannot rest. The fireman must bear the torture of his trunk for hours, not minutes; if he relaxes, even for a second, the hose will likely whip out of his hands and sweep him off the wall with a single quick twist of its violent water pressure. So the fireman eases his seat slightly, grits his teeth, and presses.

WILLIAM SANSOM
The Witnesses

A. Comprehension and Deduction

1 (a) With what is the expanse of smouldering coffee beans compared?
(b) Explain why the comparison is both accurate and effective.

2 What evidence is there in the second paragraph that the fire has now been burning for some considerable time?

3 Explain clearly, and in your own words, why the firemen must continue to play their hoses upon the beans.

4 What is the visual effect of the water being poured upon the beans and why is this so?

5 Describe, without using any form of comparison, the exact position of the fireman.

6 Explain, in your own words, the dangers involved in fire-fighting from this position.

7 What precautions does the fireman take?

8 What were the main physical discomforts of his position and how were they caused?

9 With what is the physical strain of this position compared?

10 Why is this position a greater strain than that with which it is compared?

11 (a) What action is the fireman able to take to lessen the strain?
(b) What would be the result of further action?

B. Interpretation and Criticism

1 What do the words "wreathes" and "eddies" (line 8) tell you about the movement of the fog? (Answer precisely.)

2 What is the implication of the word "seeps" (line 6) in describing the movement of the fog?

3 The following words are used by the writer in paragraph 2:

silted (line 14), promontories (line 18), quenched (line 20), erupt (line 24).

Considering each word separately, explain
(a) The usual associations of the words.
(b) Why they are aptly used in this passage.

4 Which words convey the impression, in the second half of paragraph 2, that the fire is virtually a living power, capable of reproducing itself? Why does this help to increase the tension of the description?

5 (a) Explain how, by the use of certain words in paragraph 2, the writer continues to convey the impression, first suggested in paragraph 1, that the interior of the blazing warehouse has the appearance of a landscape.

(b) How is this association maintained in paragraph 4?

6 By what means in this description does the writer convey the impression of the appalling combination of damp and heat in the beans?

C. Comment and Discussion

The questions in Section B have been entirely concerned with the vocabulary of this passage, with the meanings and implications of words, or with their connections and associations. It is the aptness of words and their implications which makes this passage so effective. Try to sum up now the reasons why the effectiveness of the description depends not on the basic situation – a warehouse fire – but on the way in which the writer, by his choice of words and detail, makes the atmosphere full of a rather sinister, frightening expectancy. (The purpose of this choice can be even better appreciated by reading the complete story.)

6 The Iron Ore Railway

In the following passage, novelist Hammond Innes recalls his experiences while on a visit to Canada in 1953 at the time of the construction of the railway from Seven Islands on the River St. Lawrence to Knob Lake in the heart of Labrador. The railway was constructed in order to transport iron ore from the vast field of deposits at Knob Lake to the St. Lawrence for export. At the time of Hammond Innes' visit, the railway was half completed and he was able to go out to work with the construction teams.

I had come to it in October, when the battle was still only half-won and the big freeze-up expected any day. The construction camps teemed with men then and the sixty miles of uncompleted grade were littered with grab cranes. Living with the engineers was like living with brigade H.Q. Head of Steel was the battle front, and it was thrust, thrust, thrust, with a target of thirty thousand tons of gravel to be shifted daily and the steel being laid at the fantastic rate of almost two miles a day; everything was on the move, camps shifting, men being
10 leap-frogged into the forward areas and the planes flying over like a bus service to keep men and machines going that were spread out all along the line of march.

I can still remember the sense of loneliness I felt as I embarked at Seven Islands in an old Dakota that carried parachute jumping wires and looked as though it had done its maiden flight in the early days of the war. It was Indian summer weather down there on the St. Lawrence, with all the country a blaze of autumn reds and the sunset a fiery conflagration fading to deep purple, and as darkness fell a fabulous
20 curtain of northern lights flung its moving folds across the stars. My companions on that flight were a strange mixture of races, from French-Canadian and Italian to Negro and Chinese – many of them bearded, and all equipped with cold-weather clothing.

In little more than an hour we had crossed the top of the 2,000-foot escarpment, a journey that only thirty or forty years back would have taken an explorer six weeks by canoe up the rapids of the Moisie river – six weeks, if he was lucky, out of the short ten-week summer, which was all the time he had if he was to get out alive. From a heat wave we flew into a blizzard, landing on an airstrip of glacial silt that was little more than a clearing in the grim silence of the jackpine forest. A truck took me into the camp, along a rutted track that was frozen hard as iron and white with a drift of snow. The camp itself was just a little huddle of huts in the stillness of the Arctic night, and the only sound in the all-pervading silence was the putter of the diesel engine that supplied the electricity. This was Camp 134, a hundred and thirty-four miles up the railway from the St. Lawrence.

And then north again by speeder, one of those little open gas-cars capable of travelling at thirty miles an hour along the completed section of the line, north through camp after camp, and every journey a bitter cold misery with hands and feet frozen and the sleet squalls coming up off the lakes with a sting in them that warned of the big freeze-up; mile after dismal mile, no change in the country — just the jackpine and the caribou moss and the lakes, the endless sombre lakes. One day I did a hundred miles—up over the height of land with the snow blowing in our faces, a husky dog sharing the tiny platform of the speeder with me. Every twenty miles or so we stopped at the cookhouse of a construction camp for scalding coffee to give us warmth, and in a lurid sunset we followed a ballast gang's rail cars to a section of double track and parked in the rear of a bunkhouse train.

It was my first construction camp meal; a hundred men crammed along the benches, and steaks and pies and dough-nuts and tinned fruit, mountains of food to be grabbed and wolfed and washed down with tea in a temperature that would have made a centrally-heated New York hotel seem like an ice house. And then on again through the blackness of the night, with the steel running out ahead like two silver threads in the speeder's headlight. I was with Gordon Racey then – a man of some fifty odd, who had come up there on a fishing trip and had stayed two and a half years as an engineer because he loved the wilds!

That was the first time I saw the siding that I was to regard as my own – a glimpse of great chunks of muskeg and caribou moss piled on the blade of a bulldozer as it struggled in the mud to make the cut that would be the switch. Every day after 70 that, for almost a week, I would leave the litter of shacks and the din of aircraft that was Camp 224, and go down with Gordon Racey to that siding. We left at seven in the morning and most times the track was so iced up that we had to use wire scrapers out ahead of the speeder. Once, and once only, the sun shone!

In that first glimpse of the siding, I had seen a lone bulldozer spearhead the attack on another stretch of Labrador's virgin soil. Before I left, the siding was complete, the grade levelled, the track laid. And after that I went on through Head of 80 Steel, past the gangs labouring to secure the ties, past the Burro crane swinging the lengths of steel into position; plodding along on foot now until there was no rail, just the brown gravel slash of the newly-levelled grade. I travelled by truck and jeep then. And later, when even the grade petered out and there was nothing to show the line of the railway but the stakes driven by the engineers through the trackless wild between the lakes, I took to helicopter and finally float plane, living all the time in camps that were either half-completed or half-dismantled, in a whirl of men constantly moving forward. 90 There were five thousand of them up there in a land where no white man had been before; men of every nationality – French and British, Canadian, Italian, Ukrainian, Polish. . . . I shared a hut one night with a German, a Nova Scotian, a Jamaican and an Egyptian-born Greek. They said if I had been there a few nights before there would have been a Chinaman as well! At one point there was an engineer from Abadan, still wearing silk scarf and khaki drill over the bulk of his woollens.

HAMMOND INNES
Harvest of Journeys

A. Comprehension and Deduction

1 Why were the construction teams working against time when the writer visited the railway?

2 (a) Why were aeroplanes a vital form of transport during this period of construction?
(b) Give proof that aeroplanes had revolutionised the speed of passenger travel in this area.

3 (a) Which forms of transport did the writer use on his journey from Seven Islands to the farthest point north?
(b) How could the writer recognise the *planned* route of the railway after he had travelled beyond the point to which track laying had advanced?

4 (a) At which Camp did the writer join the construction team?
(b) How far north of the St. Lawrence was this?

5 What definite evidence have you that some men actually worked here because they enjoyed it?

6 What was the main task performed by the construction team (from Camp 224) which the writer joined?

7 What would you consider to be the most typical features of the natural landscape through which the line was being built?

8 What would appear to be the most important piece of equipment used by construction gangs and why is this so?

9 Try to enumerate, from the evidence given here, the chief mechanical processes involved in the building of this railway.

10 What do you think the writer finds *most* unexpected amongst the groups of men he meets – according to the details given here?

B. Interpretation and Criticism

1 In the first paragraph the writer compares the construction work with a battle front. Explain in detail why this comparison is effective here.

2 By what means in the first paragraph does the writer convey a sense of restlessness and urgency?

3 What is an "Indian summer"? (line 16)

4 Two words in paragraph 3 help to tell us aboat certain features of this landscape – "escarpment" (line 26) and "rapids". (line 28) What do those words mean?

5 What are the special implications here of the word "huddle" in the phrase, "a little huddle of huts"? (line 35)

6 Which single word in paragraph 3 conveys a reasonably accurate sound impression of the action it is describing?

7 (a) What is the main task of the ballast gang?
(b) What is a "bunkhouse train"? (line 54)

8 List some of the words and phrases which make the description of the writer's first construction camp meal so virile and full-blooded and comment on why they achieve this effect.

9 Why does the writer refer to "the *litter* of shacks"? (line 70) What impression is he trying to convey?

10 Why would a siding or "switch" (line 69) be necessary at this wild spot? How does the word "switch" help you to answer this question?

11 Which phrase in paragraph 7 again suggests a comparison between this construction task and a battle?

12 Why does the writer use the word "slash" in the phrase "just the brown gravel slash of the newly-levelled grade"? (line 83) What special impression does it convey?

C. *Comment and Discussion*

1 This description reveals Hammond Innes, the explorer and writer, gathering material for future novels. Which details do you think will make good *background* material?

2 Suggest some of the possibilities for thrilling *situations* to be developed around characters and events described in this passage.

3 Give examples of Innes's style of writing here which suggest that he is probably seeing the adventure possibilities of a future novel whilst giving this account of his experiences.

4 How does his style in this passage differ from that which you would expect to find in an official report on such a project as this?

5 For a view of another landscape suitable for adventure, see Journey Across Death Valley (No. 12, page 63).

7 *The Intelligence of Cats*

No human being can know for certain what goes on in a cat's mind. "Cats are a mysterious sort of folk," said Sir Walter Scott. "There is more passing in their minds than we are aware." We humans do not like that which we cannot understand. It makes us feel uncomfortable. And many people feel uncomfortable in the presence of cats. That bland, unwinking, stare can be most disturbing. The cat looks as if it is thinking; it may be for all we know. It may even be thinking about us. Much better, much safer, to dismiss it straight away as an
10 animal of no intelligence. Many people do.

And then there are those who regard as intelligent only those animals that are obedient and have the ability to learn certain simple tricks. To such people the dog is supremely intelligent; the cat, notoriously disobedient and notoriously averse to learning the simplest trick, abysmally unintelligent.

Obedience is not necessarily a sign of intelligence, as any schoolmaster, as any sergeant-major, will tell you. Nor is the ability to perform tricks. There is a vast difference between "teachability" and intelligence. The fact that the cat is not
20 normally obedient and will not, as a rule, learn tricks does not mean that it is unintelligent.

One must consider the cat as a cat, and not as a furry human with four legs and a tail. Far too many people think of their cats like this. Cats are astonishing animals. Alone of the domestic breeds of mammals they have managed to live with Man and yet retain their independence. It is true that Man has managed to manufacture one or two breeds of domestic cat – the Smokes, for example – but he has never managed to alter the cat. Consider what he has done to the dog. He has bred
30 every conceivable shape and size, beauty and monstrosity, perfection and freak. Indeed, a visitor from Mars would find it difficult, impossible, to believe that the Dachshund and the St. Bernard, the Bulldog and the Saluki, the Pekinese and the

Great Dane were all members of one and the same species. But all domestic cats, despite their long association with Man and despite their considerable variety in colour and pattern, remain recognisably and unmistakably cats.

The cat's markedly independent nature, though it has saved him from the fate of many dogs, has also led to much mis-
40 understanding. Either you like cats or you do not like cats. There seems to be no half-way house. If you do not like cats, you may believe that they are naturally deceitful, spiteful, and sly. You will probably believe that they only make good mousers when they are half-starved. You will certainly believe that they are less intelligent than dogs.

But, if you consider the cat as a cat, and not as a sort of dog or a mirror of yourself, then you cannot fail to come to the conclusion that it is a highly intelligent animal – in all those matters which affect its own well-being. This does not mean
50 that the cat is a selfish animal – that is a purely anthropomor-phic view – it merely means that it is a remarkably sensible animal.

And you do not want to pay too much attention, if you pay any at all, to the carefully controlled experiments conducted sometimes over a period of years and designed to test the in-telligence of cats (or for that matter any other animals). They are always conducted under unnatural conditions for one thing. Man has shown that rats can be driven mad and that nervous breakdowns can be brought about in the ant. I do
60 not know what this proves. Man can also be driven mad, and modern man is very prone to nervous breakdown. All sorts of experiments have been conducted to probe the intelligence of cats. There is quite a considerable literature on the subject – some of the more important books and papers are mentioned in the bibliography – and I have read a good deal of it. This literature is entertaining, if contradictory. It proves conclu-sively that cats are highly intelligent, capable of formulating ideas, of putting two and two together, of learning a vocabu-lary of some three score human words. It proves equally con-
70 clusively that they are quite incapable of putting two and two together, quite incapable of learning anything more than their

own name (and not always that), are not in fact, intelligent at all. What this literature does prove is that some cats are more intelligent than others. And no cat lover needs to read a scientific book to learn that. There are bright cats and moron cats and dotty cats, just as there are bright men and moron men and dotty men. And that. incidentally, is equally true of dogs.

Some cats are certainly capable of learning quite astonishing things when it is to their advantage to do so. Charles Dudley Warner's Calvin used to open the hot air regulator to warm the room in which he liked to sleep. I have watched one of my own cats, Timothy, trying to turn on the switch of an electric fire. It was too stiff for him, but nobody would deny that this is putting two and two together or that Calvin was capable of doing so. A friend of mine found on two or three occasions the gas fire turned on in his study. His cat, a Blue Persian, used to sit in front of this fire when it was alight. One day he watched the cat turn the tap, sit by the fire and then walk away in disgust. And when it comes to opening doors, well, most cats are masters of the art. One could go on giving examples such as this almost for ever both from one's own experience and from the literature. They do no more than prove that the cat is highly intelligent where its own comfort or well-being is concerned. And that from the cat's point of view is all that matters.

Judged from this stand-point – and it is surely the only one to judge from – the cat's disinclination to obey is not unintelligent. You can teach a cat not to do certain things, and after due deliberation it will not do them, but in ordinary matters of obedience the cat treads its own path. This is not wilful disobedience, I am quite sure. It is not the disobedience of a naughty child. You can often see the cat sit and consider the point, and then deliberately walk away. It does not think that your ideas are as good as its own. And who is to say that it is wrong from the cat's point of view? We make the obedient dog do a lot of things that are far from good for it, and many that are dreadfully undignified.

Personally (as you will have gathered) I am, after many years of living with cats, convinced that cats are, with few

110 exceptions, most intelligent creatures, and that some are highly intelligent even for cats.

Whether they are more intelligent than dogs is another matter. Comparisons of this sort are invidious anyhow and of little or no value. One is dealing with two quite different animals. The modern dog is a man-made creature. The modern dog learns to please its master, and rarely learns anything after it is two years old. "You cannot teach an old dog new tricks" is a very true saying. The cat learns to please itself and con- tinues to learn throughout its life. That is the essential differ-
120 ence between the two.

The two together are quite delightful. I have always, since childhood, lived with cats and dogs. I have a cat and a dog now. I would not be without either. But these years of associa- tion have convinced me of one thing: that dogs brought up with cats are always a little smarter than dogs brought up with humans alone.

If you must have some comparison, then let me give you this. You can teach a dog almost anything, if you have patience. For, to the dog, Man is God, and he is very anxious to please God –
130 especially when there is the possibility of a reward in the form of food for doing so. It is impossible to teach a cat anything that he does not want to learn. For the cat does not regard Man as God. But that is not intelligence. It is wisdom.

BRIAN VESEY-FITZGERALD
Cats

A. *Comprehension and Deduction*

1 Explain in your own words why many people are uncom- fortable in the presence of cats and what their reactions often are as a result.

2 (*a*) Why do many people consider dogs to be more intelli- gent than cats?
(*b*) Explain, in your own words, why this is a dangerous assumption.

3 Which single word, used here, sums up the quality which a cat possesses but which a dog does not?

4 Why has this quality helped to make many people positively dislike cats?

5 (a) Why are present methods of measuring the intelligence of cats not really likely to produce useful results?
(b) What is the only generally acceptable conclusion reached by these tests and why, consequently, does the writer consider them rather a waste of time?

6 On what occasions are cats most likely to show intelligence?

7 Why is a cat sometimes deliberately disobedient, according to the writer?

8 What is the difference between this disobedience and that of a naughty child?

9 Explain, in your own words, why it is pointless to compare the intelligence of cats with that of dogs.

10 Why, according to the writer, do cats show a wisdom not possessed by dogs?

B. Interpretation and Criticism

1 "Only those animals that are obedient are intelligent." (lines 11-12) Using only the information in the passage, and using your own words, disprove this argument in a short paragraph.

2 Explain carefully why the word "abysmally" (line 15) implies a far greater *degree* of unintelligence than would, say, the word "extremely".

3 Why does the writer refer one to a schoolmaster or sergeant-major in stating his conclusion in lines 16-17?

4 Without using the information given in this description, but using your own examples to illustrate your explanation, explain simply the difference between "teachability" and "intelligence".

5 What does the writer mean when he says "There seems to be no half-way house"? (line 41)

6 Why can a dog be more "a mirror of yourself" (line 47) than a cat?

7 The writer states that experiments are conducted "under unnatural conditions". (line 57) What does this phrase mean? Why would it be difficult to conduct them under natural conditions?

8 What is the meaning of the statement "They are quite incapable of putting two and two together"? (line 70)

9 Why does the writer, in line 115, refer to the modern dog as "a man-made creature"? (Answer fully.)

10 What implications can be drawn from the statement: "dogs brought up with cats are always a little smarter than dogs brought up with humans alone"? (lines 124-126)

C. Comment and Discussion

1 Merely informative writing can become tedious to read, particularly if the information is not relevant to one's own needs. Discuss the methods by which Brian Vesey-Fitzgerald makes this discussion on the intelligence of cats entertaining as well as informative reading, even to those who are not necessarily cat-lovers.

2 Try to develop a group of arguments to prove that dogs, too, can possess intelligence. (Consider the exact definition of the word "intelligence".)

3 Compare the intentions of Brian Vesey-Fitzgerald in writing about animals in this passage and those of David Attenborough in writing about animals in the passage Beasts in The Bathroom (No. 3, page 11).

8 Going to the Fair

While Jones the teacher unravelled the final meanderings of *Masterman Ready*, Colin from the classroom heard another trundle of wagons and caravans rolling slowly towards the open spaces of the Forest. His brain was a bottleneck, like the wide boulevard along which each vehicle passed, and he saw, remembering last year, fresh-packed ranks of colourful Dodgem Cars, traction engines and mobile zoos, Ghost Trains and Noah's Ark figures securely crated on to drays and lorries.

So *Masterman Ready* was beaten by the prospect of more tangible distraction, though it was rare for a book of dream-adventures to be banished so easily from Colin's mind. The sum total of such free-lance wandering took him through bad days of scarcity, became a mechanical gaudily dressed pied-piper always ahead, which he would follow and one day scrag to see what made it tick. How this would come about he didn't know, didn't even try to find out – while the teacher droned on with the last few pages of his story.

Though his cousin Bert was eleven – a year older – Colin was already in a higher class at school, and felt that this counted for something anyway, even though he had found himself effortlessly there. With imagination fed by books to bursting point, he gave little thought to the rags he wore (except when it was cold) and face paradoxically overfleshed through lack of food. His hair was too short, even for a threepenny basin-crop at the barber's – which was the only thing that bothered him at school in that he was sometimes jocularly referred to as "Owd Bald-'ead".

When the Goose Fair came a few pennies had survived his weekly outlay' on comics, but Bert had ways and means of spinning them far beyond their paltry value. "We'll get enough money for lots of rides," he said, meeting Colin at the street corner of a final Saturday. "I'll show you" – putting his arm around him as they walked up the street.

" How? " Colin wanted to know, protesting: " I'm not going
to rob any shops. I'll tell you that now."

Bert, who had done such things, detected disapproval of his
past, though sensing at the same time and with a certain pride
that Colin would never have the nerve to crack open a shop at
midnight and plunge his black hands into huge jars of virgin
40 sweets. " That's not the only way to get money," he scoffed.
" You only do that when you want summat good. I'll show you
what we'll do when we get there."

Along each misty street they went, aware at every turning
of a low exciting noise from the northern sky. Bellies of cloud
were lighted orange by the fair's reflection, plain for all to see,
an intimidating bully slacking the will and drawing them
towards its heart. " If it's on'y a penny a ride then we've got
two goes each," Colin calculated with bent head, pondering
along the blank flagstoned spaces of the pavement, hands in
50 pockets pinning down his hard-begotten wealth. He was glad
of its power to take him on to roundabouts, but the thought of
what fourpence would do to the table at home filled him –
when neither spoke – with spasms of deep misery. Fourpence
would buy a loaf of bread or a bottle of milk or some stewing
meat or a pot of jam or a pound of sugar. It would perhaps
stop the agony his mother might be in from seeing his father
black and brooding by the hearth if he – Colin – had handed
the fourpence in for ten Woodbines from the corner shop. His
father would take them with a smile, get up to kiss his mother
60 in the fussy way he had and mash some tea, a happy man once
more whose re-acquired asset would soon spread to everyone
in the house.

It was marvellous what fourpence would do, if you were
good enough to place it where it rightly belonged – which I'm
not, he thought, because fourpence would also buy a fistful of
comics, or two bars of chocolate or take you twice to the flea-
pit picture-house or give you four rides on Goose Fair, and the
division, the wide dark soil-smelling trench that parted good
from bad was filled with wounds of unhappiness. And such
70 unhappiness was suspect, because Colin knew that whistling,
stone-throwing Bert at his side wouldn't put up with it for

the mere sake of fourpence – no, he'd spend it and enjoy it, which he was now out to do with half the pennies Colin had. If Bert robbed a shop or cart he'd take the food straight home – that much Colin knew – and if he laid his hands on five bob or a pound he'd give his mother one and six and say that that was all he'd been able to get doing some sort of work. But fourpence wouldn't worry him a bit. He'd just enjoy it. And so would Colin, except in the space of stillness between
80 the roundabouts.

They were close to the fair, walking down the slope of Bentinck Road, able to distinguish between smells of fish-and-chips, mussels and brandysnap. "Look on the floor," Bert called out, ever-sharp and hollow-cheeked with the fire of keeping himself going, lit by an instinct never to starve yet always looking as if he were starving. The top and back of his head was padded by overgrown hair, and he slopped along in broken slippers, hands in pockets, whistling, then swearing black-and-blue at being swept off the pavement by a tide of
90 youths and girls.

Colin needed little telling: snapped down to the gutter walked a hundred yards doubled-up like a premature rheumatic, and later shot straight holding a packet with two whole cigarettes protruding. "No whacks!" he cried, meaning: No sharing.

"Come on," Bert said, cajoling, threatening, "don't be bleedin'-well mingy, our Colin. Let's 'ave one."

Colin stood firm. Finding was keeping. "I'm saving 'em for our dad. I don't suppose 'e's got a fag to 'is name."

100 "Well, my old man ain't never got no fags either, but I wun't bother to save 'em for 'im if I found any. I mean it as well."

"P'raps we'll have a drag later on then," Colin conceded, keeping them in his pocket. They were on the asphalt path of the Forest, ascending a steep slope. Bert feverishly ripped open every cast-down packet now, chucking silver paper to the wind, slipping picture-cards in his pocket for younger brothers, crushing what remained into a ball and hurling it towards the darkness where bodies lay huddled together in some passion that

110 neither of them could understand or even remotely see the point of.

From the war memorial they viewed the whole fair, a sea of lights and tent tops flanked on two sides by dimly shaped houses whose occupants would be happy when the vast encampment scattered the following week to other towns. A soughing groan of pleasure was being squeezed out of the earth, and an occasional crescendo of squeals reached them from the Swingboats and Big Wheel as though an army were below, offering human sacrifices before beginning its march. "Let's 120 get down there," Colin said, impatiently turning over his pennies. "I want to see things. I want to get on that Noah's Ark."

ALAN SILLITOE
Noah's Ark

A. *Comprehension and Deduction*

1 What first distracted Colin's attention from *Masterman Ready*?
2 Why was he able to recognise the sounds outside?
3 Why would Colin normally have enjoyed listening to *Masterman Ready*?
4 How did reading help Colin to forget his poverty?
5 Why was Colin rather worried by Bert's plans to get more money for the fair?
6 How could the two boys tell when they were approaching the fair?
7 Why did Colin feel ashamed of spending money at the fair?
8 Explain in your own words the change which took place in Colin's father's outlook when he received cigarettes after being without.
9 Compare briefly Colin's and Bert's respective reactions to the possession of fourpence.

10 (a) Why did the two boys walk along with their eyes directed to the ground?
(b) What were the results of this?
11 What were the feelings of the local house owners towards the fair?
12 What was Colin most keen to spend his pennies on at the fair?

B. Interpretation and Criticism

1 Jones the teacher "unravelled the final meanderings of *Masterman Ready*". (lines 1-2) What do the words "unravelled" and "meanderings" suggest about the intricacies of the story at this stage? Explain the comparisons implied in these metaphors.
2 (a) What is the meaning of the word "droned"? (line 16)
(b) What does this suggest about the teacher's reading?
3 Explain more clearly what is meant by the statement: "he had found himself effortlessly there". (lines 20-21)
4 Explain what the paradox is in the statement in lines 23-24 that Colin's face was overfleshed through lack of food". (Look up the word "paradox".)
5 Why, when the boys are approaching the fair, does the writer use the word "bellies" in the phrase "Bellies of cloud"? (line 44)
6 Colin's wealth was "hard-begotten". (line 50) What does this mean?
7 Why should Colin's father be "black and brooding by the hearth"? (line 57)
8 Briefly sum up your impressions of the appearance, inside, of a typical "flea-pit picture-house" (lines 66-67), explaining the reason for the nickname.
9 What was the only possible redeeming feature of Bert's thefts of food?
10 When Colin has found the packet with two cigarettes in it, Bert tries to cajole him. (line 96) What is the meaning of "cajole"?

11 Why is the fair referred to as a "vast encampment"? (lines
114-115)

12 What is the meaning of "crescendo" in the phrase "an
occasional crescendo of squeals"? (line 117)

C. Comment and Discussion

1 This passage about Nottingham's Goose Fair naturally in-
vites comparison with Priestley's passage The Nottingham
Goose Fair (No. 4, page 16). In what ways do the two passages differ?

2 (a) What do you learn from this passage of the possible
reasons for the Goose Fair's attraction for young children?
(b) Does the information given in this passage in any way
give additional justification for J. B. Priestley's criticisms in
The Nottingham Goose Fair?

3 Alan Sillitoe is an author well able to write from his own
experience of working-class life. (See also The Fight, by Keith
Waterhouse, No. 11, page 56 and Memories, by Richard
Hoggart, No. 15, page 87.) Which aspects of this description
suggest that the writer is writing from living experience
rather than from that of an outside observer writing from
a few hours' experience or from hearsay?

4 What qualities in this passage make it more than just a
piece of dialect comedy?

5 What is the possible value of dialect in writing of this
nature?

6 Why are many "school stories" found in libraries untypical
of your school life? Compare the style of this passage with
that of the typical "school story" writer. See also Ally's
New Year's Resolution (No. 13, page 70).

9 *Memories of Christmas*

It was on the afternoon of the day of Christmas Eve, and I was in Mrs. Prothero's garden, waiting for cats, with her son Jim. It was snowing. It was always snowing at Christmas; December, in my memory, is white as Lapland, though there were no reindeer. But there were cats. Patient, cold, and callous, our hands wrapped in socks, we waited to snowball the cats. Sleek and long as jaguars and terrible-whiskered, spitting and snarling they would slink and sidle over the white back-garden walls, and the lynx-eyed hunters, Jim and I, fur-capped and moccasined trappers from Hudson's Bay off Eversley Road, would hurl our deadly snowballs at the green of their eyes. The wise cats never appeared. We were so still, Eskimo-footed arctic marksmen in the muffling silence of the eternal snows – eternal, ever since Wednesday – that we never heard Mrs. Prothero's first cry from her igloo at the bottom of the garden. Or, if we heard it at all, it was, to us, like the far-off challenge of our enemy and prey, the neighbour's Polar Cat. But soon the voice grew louder. "Fire!" cried Mrs. Prothero, and she beat the dinner-gong. And we ran down the garden, with the snowballs in our arms, towards the house, and smoke, indeed, was pouring out of the dining-room, and the gong was bombilating, and Mrs. Prothero was announcing ruin like a town-crier in Pompeii. This was better than all the cats in Wales standing on the wall in a row. We bounded into the house, laden with snowballs, and stopped at the open door of the smoke-filled room. Something was burning all right; perhaps it was Mr. Prothero who always slept there after midday dinner with a newspaper over his face; but he was standing in the middle of the room, saying "A fine Christmas!" and smacking at the smoke with a slipper.

"Call the fire-brigade," cried Mrs. Prothero as she beat the gong.

"They won't be there," said Mr. Prothero, "it's Christmas."

44

There was no fire to be seen, only clouds of smoke and Mr. Prothero standing in the middle of them, waving his slipper as though he were conducting.

"Do something," he said.

And we threw all our snowballs into the smoke – I think we missed Mr. Prothero – and ran out of the house to the
40 telephone-box.

"Let's call the police as well," Jim said.

"And the ambulance."

"And Ernie Jenkins, he likes fires."

But we only called the fire-brigade, and soon the fire-engine came and three tall men in helmets brought a hose into the house and Mr. Prothero got out just in time before they turned it on. Nobody could have had a noisier Christmas Eve. And when the firemen turned off the hose and were standing in the wet and smoky room, Jim's aunt, Miss Prothero, came down-
50 stairs and peered in at them. Jim and I waited, very quietly, to hear what she would say to them. She said the right thing, always. She looked at the three tall firemen in their shining helmets, standing among the smoke and cinders and dissolving snowballs, and she said: "Would you like something to read?"

Now out of that bright white snowball of Christmas gone comes the stocking, the stocking of stockings, that hung at the foot of the bed with the arm of a golliwog dangling over the top and small bells ringing in the toes. There was a company, gallant and scarlet but never nice to taste though I always tried
60 when very young, of belted and busbied and musketed lead soldiers so soon to lose their heads and legs in the wars on the kitchen table after the tea-things, the mince-pies, and the cakes that I helped to make by stoning the raisins and eating them, had been cleared away; and a bag of moist and many-coloured jelly-babies and a folded flag and a false nose and a tram-conductor's cap and a machine that punched tickets and rang a bell; never a catapult; once, by a mistake that no one could explain, a little hatchet; and a rubber buffalo, or it may have been a horse, with a yellow head and haphazard legs; and a
70 celluloid duck that made, when you pressed it, a most unduck-like noise, a mewing moo that an ambitious cat might make

who wishes to be a cow; and a painting-book in which I could make the grass, the trees, the sea, and the animals any colour I pleased: and still the dazzling sky-blue sheep are grazing in the red field under a flight of rainbow-beaked and pea-green birds.

Christmas morning was always over before you could say Jack Frost. And look! suddenly the pudding was burning. Bang the gong and call the fire-brigade and the book-loving firemen! Someone found the silver three-penny bit with a currant on it; and the someone was always Uncle Arnold. The motto in my cracker read:

> Let's all have fun this Christmas Day,
> Let's play and sing and shout hooray!

and the grown-ups turned their eyes towards the ceiling, and Auntie Bessie, who had already been frightened twice, by a clockwork mouse, whimpered at the side-board and had some elderberry wine. And someone put a glass bowl full of nuts on the littered table, and my uncle said, as he said once every year: "I've got a shoe-nut here. Fetch me a shoe-horn to open it, boy."

And dinner was ended.

And I remember that on the afternoon of Christmas Day, when the others sat around the fire and told each other that this was nothing, no, nothing, to the great snowbound and turkey-proud yule-log-crackling holly-berry-bedizened and kissing-under-the-mistletoe Christmas when they were children, I would go out, school-capped and gloved and mufflered, with my bright new boots squeaking, into the white world on to the seaward hill, to call on Jim and Dan and Jack and to walk with them through the silent snowscape of our town.

DYLAN THOMAS
Quite Early One Morning

A. Comprehension and Deduction

1 Where was Dylan Thomas on the afternoon of this particular Christmas Eve and what was his reason for being there?

2 (a) Who and what did Dylan and Jim imagine themselves to be on these adventures?

   (b) How did the weather help them in their imaginings?

3 (a) Why was this adventure brought to a sudden close?

   (b) What assistance were the boys able to give?

4 What did the boys do after they had given immediate help?

5 (a) Why had the boy thought that perhaps Mr. Prothero himself was on fire?

   (b) Why did Mr. Prothero see little point in calling the fire brigade?

6 (a) Which present in the Christmas stocking appealed most to the adventurous side of Dylan Thomas?

   (b) What evidence is there in the passage that it was well used?

   (c) Which present do you gain the impression that Dylan would have liked but did not receive?

7 Why did he consider the present of a hatchet to be "a mistake that no one could explain"?

8 What do you consider appealed most to Dylan in the painting books he received from the evidence given here?

9 (a) What evidence is there that Auntie Bessie suffered from practical jokers?

   (b) Why should the practical jokers choose Auntie Bessie?

10 What did Dylan do after dinner on Christmas Day?

B. Interpretation and Criticism

1 How does Dylan's description of the cats help to add to the make-believe of the boys being seasoned hunters?

2 What is the effect of the alliteration (look up the meaning of this word) in the statement "spitting and snarling they would slink and sidle"? (line 8)

3 Why are the words "slink" and "sidle" so aptly used here?

47

4 Why does Dylan place two apparently conflicting details together in the remark "from Hudson's Bay off Eversley Road"? (lines 10-11) What impression does this seemingly nonsensical remark convey?

5 Why does Dylan speak of Mrs. Prothero's "igloo" at the bottom of her garden? (line 15)

6 Why is a knowledge of what happened in Pompeii essential for the full appreciation of the simile in the statement "Mrs. Prothero was announcing ruin like a town-crier in Pompeii"? (lines 22-23) Why is the simile apt once this information is known and what does it suggest of the manner in which Mrs. Prothero spoke?

7 How does Dylan turn all the Prothero's – Mr., Mrs. and Miss – into figures of fun and even the fire into part of the comedy? (Answer carefully and in detail.)

8 Why does Dylan speak of "that bright white snowball of Christmas gone"? (line 55) Why is this such a vivid phrase?

9 What is our main memory of Dylan's painting books? Why is this memory imprinted on us almost entirely by Dylan's use of vivid colour adjectives – particularly compound adjectives? (Find out what a compound adjective is.)

10 How does the compound adjective "book-loving" used in line 79 to describe the fireman, immediately take our minds back to one happening described earlier in the passage?

11 What is the effect of the short sentence "And dinner was ended" (line 92) – and of its being placed in a paragraph on its own?

12 What is the main contrast developed in the final paragraph? In what way does the accumulation of compound adjectives in the one side of the contrast help to make the other side more effective?

C. Comment and Discussion

1 Consider the way in which this passage is written. What qualities in the writing make the style so personal – i.e. characteristic of Dylan Thomas?

2 In what ways does the style of writing suggest that this is the prose of a poet?

3 Only his untimely death prevented Dylan Thomas from following up the success of his bold experiment in writing drama solely for the medium of sound radio, " Under Milk Wood ". Much of his work, both poetry and prose, gains effect by being read aloud. This passage does. Try to explain why this should be so.

4 What are the advantages, to the dramatist and to the listener, of writing purely for *sound* radio?

10 The Night Riders

Every Saturday night, from suburban homes all over Greater London, hundreds of black-jacketed, teenage motor-cyclists move off in groups towards the M.1. Among them is one from Kingston-upon-Thames; and one of the seven members of this group is Joe Williams. He is 21 years old, has an Adam Faith haircut, the distinction of a black jacket made of leather, and he works as a builder's labourer for about £10 a week.

When his group arrives at the motorway at about the same time as the others, most of the traffic is going south, towards
10 London. Heading north, Joe's group slowly spreads out along the middle lane, and, one after the other, accelerate away. On some evenings, one or two of them will turn into the third lane and, by accelerating still more and exceeding 100 miles an hour, will "break the ton". They thus prove that they are initiates of the teenage cult called the "Ton Kids".

Joe's machine is not powerful enough to exceed 85 miles an hour, and the few times that he has done the "ton", he has been riding on a borrowed machine, soon after dawn, when the roads were almost empty of traffic. After about an hour, the
20 group have covered the full 72 miles of the motorway and turn back towards London again. By now, the evening's sport is usually over, and the run back is taken at a steady 50 miles an hour. At the other end of the M.1., they turn towards Watford and follow the neon signs to an enormous, glass-fronted transport cafe, the "Busy Bee". Outside there are a few cars, a few coaches, and long rows of shining black and chrome motorcycles.

It is now eleven o'clock at night. Inside, a long queue of "Ton Kids" wait for tea and egg and chips, and about 50 are
30 already sitting down talking about motor-cycles. Standing out from this crowd – except for the odd coach party – are a few moderately dressed tourists, who have come along after closing time in the pubs to see what "coffee-bar cowboys" look like in

the flesh. Openly ignored, the tourists are bitterly resented in private conversation. They have come to the "Busy Bee" with wild stories of teenage recklessness, and some have been advised not to visit it for fear that the "cowboys" will beat them up.

They watch, with both impatience and trepidation, either for a fight or a display of dangerous skill like the "roundabout game". This is allegedly played by putting a record on the juke box, rushing out to a motor-cycle, starting it, roaring off round a nearby roundabout, and returning to one's original position before the record ends. This requires an average speed of more than eighty miles an hour, and it is easier to find people who have friends who have seen it than to find actual witnesses.

All the "Ton Kids" who were interviewed in the "Busy Bee" on a recent Saturday night believed that the "round-about game" was an impossible one. Although it might have been attempted once or twice, they said, most of the stories about it were nothing but an example of the hostile campaign which is being conducted against teenagers on motor-cycles. The teenagers there were extremely worried by the campaign. They thought it was removing what little tolerance the public ever had for them, and after some discussion Joe Williams was appointed to express their point of view.

"Public opinion is really turning against us," he said. "People in cars, even old blokes on motor-bikes, shake their fists at us as we go past. The police try to pull us in for the smallest things. I don't know what they're trying to prove when they do that, but their attitude doesn't help anybody. When people see a teenager on a motor-bike, they think he must be mad. They'll believe anything about us, so long as it's bad enough. A kid was killed the other day. He was going down a steep hill with two hairpin bends in it, and he slipped and went underneath a lorry coming up. A witness said he was doing the 'ton' down the hill, but it's just impossible. You can't get as far down as he did going faster than 35. But if you say the witness was lying you won't get anywhere, because nobody will take any notice.

"The public doesn't seem to realise that it takes skill to ride a bike and that we've been practising for years. The real curses aren't us. They're the car drivers. The other day, I was waiting at some traffic lights next to a vicar. When the lights changed, he swung his car right out in front of me, and he would have had me on the ground if I hadn't been watching it. He probably talks about teenage hooligans in his sermons, but he's the sort who ought to be banned. The only thing you
80 can do is to keep away from cars as much as possible.

"Only about 10 per cent of kids who ride bikes are these 'coffee-bar cowboys', but they're the ones who talk all the time and get us all a bad name. Most of the things they talk about, they never do anyway. Most of them don't even have bikes which can do the 'ton'.

"I only know one kid who doesn't wear a crash helmet. He says it's chicken. He takes off from here so fast that his front wheel doesn't touch the ground till he's on the road. Everybody here thinks he's stupid. He'll fracture his skull soon, and
90 we all know it. Not that I haven't done the 'ton'. I haven't done it on the motorway either; that's too boring. I've been in one or two burn-ups as well. That's when you're going along and a kid overtakes you. Then you overtake him, then he overtakes you again, and so on. I don't do that now; you only have to come off once to stop yourself doing it again.

"I live for motor-bikes. I don't like my work. I do it for the money and spend it all on the bike. I've only got eight bob left for the whole of next week. A teenager's life is really boring these days and motor-bikes have real kicks. The Govern-
100 ment ought to do something for teenagers. Youth Clubs are no good. Why do they think I'm interested in carpentry and sing-songs?

"So I come here all the time I can. You get a thrill out of going fast and it's healthy being in the open air like that. It makes you feel good to get dressed up, too, in the black jacket and the boots and the crash helmet with badges all over it. I want a bigger bike now. When you've got a motor-bike you're never satisfied with it; those things really grip you. I don't care what the papers say or what the public thinks, I want a bigger

110 bike and I'm going to get one. It'll set me back about £300 –
more than six months' wages.

"I suppose we'll all grow out of it and settle down one day.
I want to start my own business eventually, but I'm not ready
for it yet. You've got to have fun while you're young."

The fact remained, he admitted, that too many teenagers do
have serious accidents on motor-cycles, but he thought he had
the solution. Nobody should be allowed to have a big machine
until they are experienced with a small one, like him. That
would stop 16-year-olds, who are the ones, he claims, who have
120 the bad accidents from trying to control a powerful machine
they didn't understand.

After a final cup of tea he went outside to his machine. He
carefully fitted his helmet on to his head, and with the greatest
possible display of restraint he slid slowly into the traffic. To
show how careful he was, he went so slowly that he tended to
wobble.

The Guardian

A. Comprehension and Deduction

1 What is the most distinctive feature of the appearance of
these motor-cyclists?

2 What is the main object of their evening's enjoyment?

3 What is normally the main difference between their north-
bound and southbound run on the M.1.?

4 For what purpose do late evening trippers visit the "Busy
Bee" and why are they disliked by the motor-cyclists?

5 (a) What do the trippers *most* hope to see happen on their
late night visits?
(b) Why are they likely to be disappointed?
(c) What do the motor-cyclists consider to be the purpose of
the publicity given to this alleged display?

6 What evidence does Joe Williams produce to justify his

argument that the public are conducting a campaign against young motor-cyclists?

7 (a) Why is Williams particularly critical of the real " coffee-bar cowboys"?

(b) What proof does he give that even their stories are exaggerated?

8 Why did Joe choose a different road from the M.1. on which to do the "ton"?

9 What now prevented Joe from taking part in "burn-ups"?

10 Explain fully, in your own words, all the reasons for Joe's love of motor-cycling.

11 What proof do you find in Joe's comments that, although he loves adventure and a certain amount of risk-taking, he has little sympathy with sheer foolhardiness?

12 Why did Joe depart with such extreme care?

B. Interpretation and Criticism

1 (a) What is a "cult"? (line 15)

(b) What are "initiates"? (line 15)

(c) What form did the *initiation ceremony* take in the case of the "Ton Kids"?

2 What are neon signs? (line 24)

3 Why does the writer use the words "moderately dressed" to describe the tourists who visit "The Busy Bee"? (line 32)

4 Which word in paragraph 5 suggests that the tourists are not completely at ease in this cafe?

5 What is implied by the word "allegedly" in the statement "This is allegedly played . . ."? (line 41)

6 What is implied by the use of the word "hostile" to describe the campaign being conducted against youthful motor cyclists? (line 52)

7 Why does Joe Williams particularly quote the example of a vicar in his attack on poor car drivers?

8 Without quoting Joe's example of the Youth Club, try to explain why teenagers should be critical of efforts made by the Government to provide facilities for their entertainment.

9 Try to explain clearly the reason for the appeal to many youths of (*a*) motor-bikes and (*b*) the dress used for motor-cycling.

10 What evidence is there in Joe's remarks that he realises that his love of motor-bikes is probably only a youthful enthusiasm?

C. *Comment and Discussion*

1 Newspaper articles sometimes reveal bias on the part of their writers. Do you feel that this article shows bias for or against The Night Riders or is it reasonably impartial? Justify your conclusion.

2 This is a piece of good journalism. Journalistic techniques differ from purely literary techniques. Can you find any points of style or vocabulary in this article which indicate that it was written as a journalistic rather than as a purely literary effort? What must a journalist bear in mind when writing for newspaper readers?

3 A feature of journalistic writing is often the " live quote ". Compare the styles of writing before and after Joe Williams takes over.

(*a*) How do they differ?

(*b*) Does the technique of live quotation here add to the article's readability?

(*c*) Does it help to present an impartial case or not?

Give reasons for your answer.

4 Why is extensive use made of the "quote" in journalism?

5 For another example of good journalism see Steam's Last Mileposts (No. 16, page 94).

_11_ _The Fight_

The whole school knew about the fight next morning. I was
a bit frightened in case any of the teachers got to know
about it, but proud in a way because I was so famous. All day
me and Raymond Garnett kept out of each other's way. I
thought I could beat him with one hand tied behind my back,
but as the day wore on I started getting like a sinking feeling
and wanting to go to the lavatory all the time. I didn't want to
go back to school after dinner and I wished I could break my
leg. But I knew I would have to go, and on the way back to
10 school Ted shouted after me. "Have you made your will
out?"

Anyway, that afternoon while we were having geography I
was balancing my inkwell on the edge of my desk and it went
and tipped up and spilt ink all over the floor. Old Ma Bates
was taking us that afternoon and she was in a bad temper. She
went: "You clumsy article! Now you stay in after four o'clock
and wipe it up! ' I felt as though a lead weight had been lifted
out of my stomach and I breathed in heavily. Next to me Ted
whispered: "Needn't think you're getting away with it, cos
20 you're not! " But there was a chance, though. For all I knew
Old Ma Bates would keep me in till half-past four.

The bell went for going-home time and Old Ma Bates said
everyone could go. I thought for a minute she was going to
forget about keeping me in, but she didn't. "You get to and
clean that mess! " she said. Ted whispered: "We'll be waiting
for you, so don't try to get away."

I started mopping at the floor with bits of old blotting
paper, soaking the ink in as slowly as I could. Old Ma Bates
sat at her desk marking exercise books. Once I looked up and
30 saw Ted and Little Rayner peering in through the French
windows. Ted was pretending to slit his throat with his finger.
Soon they went away. I finished cleaning up the ink off the

56

floor and sat at my desk with my arms folded, hoping Old Ma Bates wouldn't look up.

It must have been about quarter-past four when she closed her exercise books and said: "You can go now, and don't let me catch you touching those inkwells again!" I walked slowly out of the class room, down the corridor and out of the main entrance with "BOYS" printed up over it in stone, through the
40 half-closed trellis gates and into the playground. At first it looked as though the others had gone but then I saw them all standing up near the railings – Ted, Little Rayner, Mono and Raymond Garnett.

"Thought he wouldn't come out!" said Little Rayner.

"Has he got his coffin with him?" said Ted.

We walked out of the playground and round by Parkside towards the fighting field. We walked without saying anything. The only one who spoke was Ted who said: "Got any chewy?" to Little Rayner, and that was the only thing that
50 was said.

I was frightened when we got down on to the field, not by Raymond Garnett but by this big crowd of kids who had waited to see the fight. At the same time I was happy because they were waiting to see me and Raymond Garnett and nobody else.

There was a big ring of kids round the grey patch that was worn in the grass, where the fights were always held. They parted to let us through, and looking round I saw hundreds of other kids teeming on to the field after us, some of them
60 running. Little Rayner shoves his way to the front, singing: "Whipsey diddle-de-dandy-dee," this stupid song we had to learn at school.

I had never had a fight before. I felt important and pleased at the crowds who were round us, none of them touching us but leaving it to us to have our fight.

"Back a bit," I said, and I was right pleased when they moved back. I took off my coat and handed it to a kid I did not know. He took it and held it carefully over his arm, and this pleased me too.
70 Raymond Garnett took off his coat and his glasses. I had

never seen him without his glasses before, except that time when we were playing in Clarkson's woods with Marion. He had a white mark over his nose where he had taken them off and it gave me the feeling that I could bash him easy. He gave them to a kid to look after and as the crowd started pushing the kid went: " Mi-ind his glasses! "

We both stepped forward to meet each other and put our fists up. We stood staring at each other and dancing round a bit like they do on the pictures, then I shot out my right 80 hand to Garnett's chin but it missed and caught his shoulder. The next thing I knew was that his fist had caught me a sting-ing clout over the forehead. I was surprised and worried at the size of the blow and I began to notice, in a far-off sort of way, that he was a lot bigger than me and that his arms were thicker and longer.

I don't know how I got time to look at the people in the ring around us, but I did, and I noticed that I didn't even know most of them. Little Rayner was at the front shouting: " Go it, Garno! " and this hurt me, don't ask me why. Ted 90 was at the back, jumping up and down to get a good look.

I started trying to remember what people had told me about fighting. I knew you had to hit a man on his shoulders so as to weaken his arms, and another trick was to pretend to hit him in the belly and then when his arms went down, well you get him in the face instead. They didn't work. I hit Garno twice on his right shoulder and he didn't feel anything, and when I tried to go for his belly my own arms were down and he hit me on the lip. I could feel it swelling already and I heard the crowd go: " Ohhhhh! " I suddenly realised that I had 100 made a mistake and that Garno was tougher than I was and he was going to wipe the blinking floor with me and there was nothing I could do about it.

I remember reading in the *Hotspur* or somewhere about all these boxers, they always hit with their left. I tried to hit Garno with my left hand but I couldn't aim it properly and I missed. Little Rayner started going: " Cur, call this a fight! " One or two kids at the back had started their own little fights.

I started trying to look into Garno's eyes all the time. This

was something else I remembered. If you look the other man
in the eyes all the time, well you can tell what he's going to
do.

You couldn't tell what blinking Garno was going to do. He
seemed surprised that I was staring at him all the time, and
for a minute I thought he was going to start saying: "Have
you seen all?" His mouth was pursed up and he looked as
though he was getting his mad up. Suddenly, for no reason
at all as far as I could see, he went: "Right! You've asked for
it now!" and he started laying in to me. I started dancing
round backwards like proper boxers do. There was a bump or
a stone or something and I tripped over it and fell, sprawling.
Little Rayner shouted: "What you doing on the floor, man?"
Garno stood over me, breathing through his mouth.

"Do you give in?" he said.

The question seemed cocky and unfair. I said: "We haven't
started yet!" I got up on my feet and he hit me with his fist
in the face. I didn't fall this time but I turned round to stop
him hitting me. I was all hunched up and almost cringing and
I could feel his knuckles on the back of my head. Some kids
were drifting away from the back of the crowd and that was
even worse. Ted at the back started shouting: "One-two-three-
four, who-are-we-for-GARno!" Nobody took up the cry and he
sounded silly.

Garno had stopped moving round the ring now. He just
stood there and every time I came near him he hit me. He hit
me in the lip again and it started bleeding.

We stood staring at each other, our fists clenched, breathing
heavily. I said to the kid who had my coat: "Get us my
hanky," because the blood was going down my chin.

The kid said: "Clean your boots for fourpence." He
dropped my coat on the floor and started going: "Yurrrks!"
as though it were all over lice or something.

"Do you give in?" said Raymond Garnett.

I didn't answer him, I couldn't. Suddenly Garno lifted his
hand and slapped me across the cheek. It wasn't with his fist,
it was with his open hand. I had to bite into my bleeding lip
to stop myself from crying. The tears came into my eyes.

"So-ock him, man!" said Little Rayner.

"Do you give in?" said Raymond Garnett. He slapped me across the face again. I couldn't stop the tears rolling down 150 my cheeks.

"Yer," I muttered.

KEITH WATERHOUSE
There is a Happy Land

A. Comprehension and Deduction

1 In what ways did Ted frighten the writer and in what ways did he make sure that the writer did not get a chance to withdraw, before the fight began?

2 What proof have you that the writer did not want to take part in the fight? (Answer fully.)

3 Why did the writer feel relieved when he tipped over the inkwell?

4 Explain, in your own words, why the writer felt happier about the fight when he reached the field. In what ways was his confidence built up a little before the fight began?

5 Which events in the early part of the fight made him begin to lose his confidence?

6 (*a*) Which boxing tips did the writer try to carry out?
   (*b*) Explain why they failed.

7 (*a*) What evidence is there that the crowd began to find the fight boring?
   (*b*) Why should they find it boring, do you think?

8 What event suggested that Raymond Garnett was merely conserving his strength in the first stages of the fight?

9 (*a*) When do you think that Raymond Garnett became fully confident of victory?
   (*b*) What proof does he give?
   (*c*) What proof is there that the crowd is of the same opinion?

10 What action of Raymond Garnett's upset the writer most? Why? Why did Raymond Garnett do this?
11 How was the victor decided in these fights?

B. Interpretation and Criticism

1 Comment on Ted's sense of humour in this passage. What do his humorous remarks and general behaviour reveal about his character and about his attitude to the writer?
2 What impression do you gain of Little Rayner's character from his comments and behaviour? How does he reveal his sympathies in the fight and what effect does this have on the writer?
3 Why did the writer attend carefully to the preliminaries before the fight? Why were they of special importance to him?
4 Analyse carefully the part played by the crowd in this event, noting particularly the various effects of its behaviour on the writer.
5 Sum up your impressions of the social background of the boys in this description.

C. Comment and Discussion

1 You will have noted that there are no vocabulary questions in the section "Interpretation and Criticism". This passage has been written using the straightforward vocabulary likely to be used by the boy at the actual time of his experiences.

(a) Is this method of telling the story successful?
(b) By its use of simple, sometimes dialect vocabulary, does the passage become more lifelike so that its local setting can be appreciated by readers anywhere? Give reasons for your answer.
(c) Alternatively, does its local style automatically restrict enjoyment to those readers acquainted with Yorkshire?
2 Consider the qualities which a "regional" story must possess to have a national or international appeal.

3 Here we have been dealing with an extract from a novel. Academically speaking the style is open to criticism. But a novel can still be highly regarded without necessarily possessing an academically correct style. Why is this? What are the essential ingredients of a good modern novel?

4 Reconsider particularly in view of your studies of this passage, the passages by Alan Sillitoe, Going to the Fair (No. 8, page 38) and J. B. Priestley, The Goose Fair (No. 4, page 16).

12 Journey Across Death Valley

Presently he turned the last corner that obstructed sight of Death Valley. Tappan had never been appalled by any aspect of the desert, but it was certain that here he halted. Back in his mountain-walled camp the sun had passed behind the high domes, but here it still held most of the valley in its blazing grip. Death Valley looked a ghastly, glaring level of white, over which a strange dull leaden haze drooped like a blanket. Ghosts of mountain peaks appeared to show dim and vague. There was no movement of anything. No wind. The valley
10 was dead. Desolation reigned supreme. Tappan could not see far toward either end of the valley. A few miles of white glare merged at last into leaden pall. A strong odour, not unlike sulphur, seemed to add weight to the air.

    Tappan strode on, mindful that Jenet had decided opinions of her own. She did not want to go straight ahead or to right or left, but back. That was the one direction impossible for Tappan. And he had to resort to a rare measure – that of beating her. But at last Jenet accepted the inevitable and headed down into the stark and naked plain. Soon Tappan
20 reached the margin of the zone of shade cast by the mountain and was now exposed to the sun. The difference seemed tremendous. He had been hot, oppressed, weighted. It was now as if he was burned through his clothes, and walked on red-hot sands.

    When Tappan ceased to sweat and his skin became dry, he drank half a canteen of water, and slowed his stride. Inured to desert hardship as he was, he could not long stand this. Jenet did not exhibit any lessening of vigour. In truth what she showed now was an increasing nervousness. It was almost
30 as if she scented an enemy. Tappan never before had such faith in her. Jenet was equal to this task.

    With that blazing sun on his back, Tappan felt he was being pursued by a furnace. He was compelled to drink the remaining half of his first canteen of water. Sunset would save him. Two more hours of such insupportable heat would lay him prostrate.

The ghastly glare of the valley took on a reddish tinge. The heat was blinding Tappan. The time came when he walked beside Jenet with a hand on her pack, for his eyes could no
40 longer endure the furnace glare. Even with them closed he knew when the sun sank behind the Panamints. That fire no longer followed him. And the red left his eyelids.

With the sinking of the sun the world of Death Valley changed. It smoked with heat veils. But the intolerable constant burn was gone. The change was so immense that it seemed to have brought coolness.

In the twilight – strange, ghostly, sombre, silent as death – Tappan followed Jenet off the sand, down upon the silt and borax level, to the crusty salt. Before dark Jenet halted at a
50 sluggish belt of fluid – acid, it appeared to Tappan. It was not deep. And the bottom felt stable. But Jenet refused to cross. Tappan trusted her judgement more than his own. Jenet headed to the left and followed the course of the strange stream.

Night intervened. A night without stars or sky or sound, hot, breathless, charged with some intangible current! Tappan dreaded the midnight furnace winds of Death Valley. He had never encountered them. He had heard prospectors say that any man caught in Death Valley when these gales blew would never get out to tell the tale. And Jenet seemed to have some-
60 thing on her mind. She was no longer a leisurely, complacent burro. Tappan imagined Jenet seemed stern. Most assuredly she knew now which way she wanted to travel. It was not easy for Tappan to keep up with her, and ten paces beyond him she was out of sight.

At last Jenet headed the acid wash, and turned across the valley into a field of broken salt crust, like the roughened ice of a river that had broken and jammed, then frozen again. Impossible was it to make even a reasonable headway. It was a zone, however, that eventually gave way to Jenet's instinct
70 for direction. Tappan had long ceased to try to keep his bearings. North, south, east, and west were all the same to him. The

night was a blank – the darkness a wall – the silence a terrible menace flung at any living creature. Death Valley had endured them millions of years before living creatures had existed. It was no place for a man.

Tappan was now three hundred and more feet below sea level, in the aftermath of a day that had registered one hundred and forty-five degrees of heat. He knew, when he began to lose thought and balance – when only the primitive instincts 80 directed his bodily machine. And he struggled with all his will power to keep hold of his sense of sight and feeling. He hoped to cross the lower level before the midnight gales began to blow.

Tappan's hope was vain. According to record, once in a long season of intense heat, there came a night when the furnace winds broke their schedule, and began early. The misfortune of Tappan was that he had struck this night.

Suddenly it seemed that the air, sodden with heat, began to move. It had weight. It moved soundlessly and ponderously. 90 But it gathered momentum. Tappan realised what was happening. The blanket of heat generated by the day was yielding to outside pressure. Something had created a movement of the hotter air that must find its way upward, to give place for the cooler air that must find its way down.

Tappan heard the first, low, distant moan of wind and it struck terror to his heart. It did not have an earthly sound. Was that a knell for him? Nothing was surer than the fact that the desert must sooner or later claim him as a victim. Grim and strong, he rebelled against the conviction.

100 That moan was a forerunner of others, growing louder and longer until the weird sound became continuous. Then the movement of wind was accelerated and began to carry a fine dust. Dark as the night was, it did not hide the pale sheets of dust that moved along the level plain. Tappan's feet felt the slow rise in the floor of the valley. His nose recognised the zone of borax and alkali and nitre and sulphur. He had reached the pit of the valley at the time of the furnace winds.

The moan augmented to a roar, coming like a mighty storm through a forest. It was hellish – like the woeful tide of

110 Acheron. It enveloped Tappan. And the gale bore down in tremendous volume, like a furnace blast. Tappan seemed to feel his body penetrated by a million needles of fire. He seemed to dry up. The blackness of night had a spectral, whitish cast; the gloom was a whirling medium; the valley floor was lost in a sheeted, fiercely seeping stream of silt. Deadly fumes swept by, not lingering long enough to suffocate Tappan. He would gasp and choke – then the poison gas was gone on the gale. But hardest to endure was the heavy body of moving heat. Tappan grew blind, so that he had to hold on to Jenet, and
120 stumble along. Every gasping breath was a tortured effort. He could not bear a scarf over his face. His lungs heaved like great leather bellows. His heart pumped like an engine short of fuel. This was the supreme test for his never proven endurance. And he was all but vanquished.

Tappan's senses of sight and smell and hearing failed him. There was left only the sense of touch – a feeling of rope and burro and ground – and an awful insulating pressure upon all his body. His feet marked a change from salty plain to sandy ascent and then to rocky slope. The pressure of wind gradually
130 lessened: the difference in air made life possible; the feeling of being dragged endlessly by Jenet had ceased. Tappan went his limit and fell into oblivion.

When he came to, he was suffering bodily tortures. Sight was dim. But he saw walls of rocks, green growths of mesquite, tamarack, and grass. Jenet was lying down, with her pack flopped to one side. Tappan's dead ears recovered to a strange murmuring, babbling sound. Then he realised his deliverance. Jenet had led him across Death Valley, up into the mountain range, straight to a spring of running water.

ZANE GREY
Tappan's Burro

A. Comprehension and Deduction

1 Why was the sun still shining in the valley but not back at the camp he had just left?

2 (a) What was Jenet's reaction when they reached the spot from which they were to cross Death Valley?
(b) How did Tappan deal with this?

3 At what point did the heat suddenly become even more intense?

4 In which direction was Tappan crossing Death Valley to begin with? How can you tell this?

5 Why did Tappan dismount from Jenet?

6 Why did Tappan not make Jenet cross the stream which looked like acid?

7 What did Tappan fear most in Death Valley at this time? Why?

8 Geographically, which are the most unusual physical and climatic features of Death Valley? (Use only information given in this passage.)

9 Explain simply and in your own words why the hot winds blew at night in Death Valley.

10 What were the most dangerous features of the winds as far as humans were concerned?

11 Why was Tappan's worst fear in his journey across Death Valley realised?

12 Sum up the chief physical effects of the furnace winds on Tappan.

13 Explain the ways in which Tappan was dependent on Jenet throughout this journey.

14 Outline the changes in surface which could be noted in this journey across Death Valley.

15 What information do you gather about the landscape on either side of Death Valley?

B. Interpretation and Criticism

1 "A strange dull leaden haze dropped *like a blanket*." (line 7) Explain why the simile is appropriate here.

2 What is the effect of the writer's use of a group of short sentences in the first paragraph?

3 What combination of effects caused the tremendous *glare* in Death Valley before sunset?

4 Explain the statement " It smoked with heat veils ". (line 44)

5 What does the word "sluggish" tell you about the movement of the acid-like stream? (line 50)

6 What were "prospectors" and for what might they have been prospecting? (line 57)

7 What does the word "complacent" suggest about Jenet's nature under more normal conditions? (line 60)

8 Why is there a salt crust in Death Valley?

9 Look up the meaning of the word "paradox". Why is the simile "like the roughened ice of a river that had broken and jammed, then frozen again" (lines 66-67) effective in a paradoxical way here?

10 What were "the primitive instincts" which "directed his bodily machine" (lines 79-80) and what was the unspoken message which they probably conveyed to Tappan?

11 What is paradoxical about the word "sodden" in the phrase "sodden with heat" (line 88) used to describe the night air?

12 What is the meaning of the word "knell" in the question "Was that a knell for him?" (line 97) d what is its sinister implication?

13 What is the meaning of "augmented" in the statement "The moan augmented to a roar"? (line 108) Which word is the exact opposite of "augmented"?

14 Express in more modern English the statement "He was all but vanquished". (line 124)

15 Express in more modern English the statement "Tappan went his limit and fell into oblivion." (lines 131-132)

C. *Comment and Discussion*

1 Adventure stories often rely to a considerable extent on coincidence. What part does coincidence play in this

particular episode, firstly in producing a nasty situation, secondly in producing a happy ending?

2 Zane Grey was one of the pioneer writers of " Westerns ". In what ways does the landscape of the West provide an ideal setting for tales of adventure? To what extent has this helped the Western to become popular and to what extent are typical Western characters also important ingredients?

3 Compare the adventure possibilities of this landscape with other good settings, such as Dartmoor, the jungle, the frozen north. Re-read The Iron Ore Railway (No. 6, page 26).

4 How does the manner in which this passage is written and the words and phrases used, help to achieve the main aims of this type of story – to thrill and to excite?

13 Ally's New Year Resolution

Gloria Berners lay asleep in her bed at 49 Magnolia Buildings. She was fourteen years old and had been christened Gloria Evelyn, but the other children had always called her Glory Alleluia, and this had become Ally for short.

"New Year's Day!" said Ally to herself as she woke up. "Got to wish for something." She turned over on the pillow, and her mop of curly yellow hair made a fan round her face. She thought about the things she wanted. The first one was to get Doreen out of her bed for good. That would be grand.

10   Doreen snorted in her sleep like a little pig.

She gave Doreen a good bump with her behind to stop her snoring.

Have a room to myself, that's next, she thought. Be glamorous like film stars. Meet Elvis Presley or Tommy Steele. Have some proper high heel shoes. Go to the Riviera for a holiday and wear a bikini.

That's too many wishes for one year, Ally said to herself. Fat lot of hope getting any of them. Not a chance of a room to myself, let alone a holiday on the Riviera.

20   No one had a room to themselves at 49 Magnolia Buildings. The buildings were a block of old-fashioned flats. Mum and Dad shared a room, the boys, Val and Len, who were twelve and eight, slept together, while Doreen, Ally and Auntie Glad were in the third room. Not that Auntie Glad was much bother. She was so quiet and so small, almost a dwarf. When her mother had died, she had brought her own bed to Magnolia Buildings with her, and her trunk had just fitted under it. She took up very little cubic space at all. Nor did she speak at meals, but just slipped in and out to her dressmaking job, and no one

30   ever noticed her.

But the boys took up all her share of space. Val was like twelve elephants. He never moved without carrying the entire landscape with him. Len played trains all over the floor. As for Doreen, there were her books on every table. She had to take her Eleven Plus exam this month. You would have thought she was the only girl in the world to take it, judging by the fuss she made. She's just cut out for a teacher, thought Ally.

40   Then Ally remembered her diary. She must start to write it. Lou, her friend, had given her one for Christmas. Lou was going to keep a diary too, so that they could compare notes about all the exciting things that happened during the year. Ally lay and thought of the things she would write. This first day of the year was dark and snowing. Luckily it was a Saturday, and Dad was laid off for weekends as things were slack. Breakfast could be late.

Auntie Glad dressed under her nightgown in the dark and went off to wash in the scullery. The only water in the flat was there, and the bath was under the kitchen table.

50   Ally turned on the light and opened her diary. She wrote: " Hullo New Year. Aren't you cold? We all live here in the flat. Mum, Dad and Auntie Glad, Me, Val, Doreen and Len. Auntie Glad came to live here when Dad's mum died. I wished for a lot of things this morning, but won't get them. I heard Mum go out to work at five. She is still cleaning offices but will be back for breakfast. Dad works on the railway. I must make the morning tea . . ."

She went to put the kettle on when Auntie Glad came back to do her hair. They did not speak to each other. There was 60   nothing to say at half-past seven in the morning. It was too cold. Auntie Glad began taking out her curlers.

The kitchen smelt stuffy. Ally put on the hot water, then some cups and saucers on a tray and buttered a few slices of bread. Auntie Glad ate no breakfast, but she would be glad of a cup of tea.

Then Ally went to call the boys. They were both asleep in the one bed, with only Val's black curls and Len's crew cut showing above the sheet. Their clothes were flung on the floor, all mixed up with their dirty boots.

70   " Wake up," shouted Ally. " It's New Year's Day. And mind you wash! "

They did not stir. She shook Val. Glamour, she thought, what a hope! Picking up all the clothes off the floor, she threw them on top of the boys.

Val opened his eyes and shut them again. It was too cold to move. He could tell that by the tip of his nose. New Year's Day, he thought, perhaps this year I'll get my bike.

Dad was now shaving at the sink. It was like a jigsaw puzzle to fit in all the activities of the scullery. To an observer, the
80 Berners family might seem to be performing a complicated dance as they washed, shaved, cleaned teeth and cooked meals. Ally laid breakfast for six while Auntie Glad slipped across the room and out of the door like a small grey mouse. No one saw her go. All she had done was to leave an empty cup with a few tea leaves in it.

Mum came back and the day really began. " Cor, you ought to have been with us girls this morning," she cried as she opened the door. " Laugh! We nearly died. There was ice everywhere and the bus skidding about. We had that fat con-
90 ductor. He's a scream! Kept us all in fits. Mrs. Beagle, she works in Shell, she gave as good as she got. Come on, let's have a cuppa. I'm dying for one."

That was Mum all over, bringing the frosty morning and the jokes of the other cleaners home with her. She was always laughing and talking and always ready to sit down and have a cup of tea. Being stout these days, she was glad to take the weight off her feet. If the flat was usually rather untidy, well what of it?

" The house is made for the people, not the people for the
100 house," Mum would say, gathering up an armful of clothes and toys and shoving them into the nearest drawer. " There's some as would rather have the room to the dirt that's brought in, but I like a bit of company and a bit of fun. Come on, fill up and don't spare the sugar! "

There were always friends and neighbours sitting in Mum's flat. They came there to be cheered up and made to laugh. There's no marble halls about this place, thought Ally. but Mum makes it O.K.

" You got them trousers on again, Al? " asked Mum and

110 she burst out laughing. "Never saw such a lot as you girls are! We wore their faces in lockets, but you've got to have their names worked on your pants." This was all because Ally had embroidered the names of Elvis Presley and Tommy Steele down the outsides of her blue jeans.

"All the other girls did it too," she said, cross at being mocked. "It's the fashion."

"Stand on your heads, you lot would, if it was the fashion," said Mum. "Well, this won't keep baby. I must get a move on. You all going to the pictures this morning?"

120 On Saturdays, the children all went to the cheap show at the cinema. It cost them only sixpence.

"I'm not going. I'm busy," said Val.

Mum smiled and hoped he was not getting into mischief again. He was a good-looking boy with curly hair and dark eyes who was going to be tall. Val was usually in trouble.

"I'm going up to the pond to see if there's ice," cried Len.

"Get out!" shouted Val. He always shouted, never talked. "They won't let you on the ice. They break it up so us boys can't slide. Rotten, I call it. What's ice for?"

130 "They don't want you getting drowned," said Dad. He was a big fair man with a droopy moustache. He never said much as it was impossible to out-talk Mum when she got started. Now he settled down to do his pools. Doreen said she had to make a map of Europe.

"I don't want to go to the pictures, Mum." Ally sounded sulky. "It's kid stuff. Cowboys riding round that same old village. And who wants to see Micky Mouse?"

"I do," piped up Len. His pointed little nose was red with the cold. "Oh Mum, I do want to go. Or I'll miss the serial,

140 THE BLACK BOX. It's ever so exciting. Last time, the monster man was in a dark cave and . . ."

"Go on, Ally, take him, do," said Mum. "I'm not having him crossing the High Street on his own."

"Should think not," said Dad.

"You go on now, Ally, and do the shopping, and then take Len."

"It's a waste of money," grumbled Ally. "I want to go and

see A HEART FOR A CORONET next Wednesday. Now, that'll be a smashing picture."

150   "I'll pay for you to go, if you'll just take Len now," wheedled Mum.

Dad said, "That's right. Chucking your money away!"

"That's what I work for, isn't it?" cried Mum with spirit, her black eyes sparking. "So as to have a bit of money I can chuck away, and you not able to throw it in my teeth."

She liked spoiling the children and waiting on them. She had spoilt them all, especially Len. But none of the family could resist Len, with his dimples, his funny nose and his mouse-coloured crew cut.

160   "Mum never goes to the pictures ever," said Doreen in an accusing voice to Ally.

"Shut up," shouted Ally. "Give me the basket. What do you want, Mum?"

Ally usually liked shopping. She was friends with everyone in the shops, and they often gave her a scrap more meat or an extra apple. But this morning she felt sour. It was New Year's Day, and something wonderful ought to be happening. Something with a spot of glamour.

Outside, the air was sparkling and full of frost. It was an
170   exhilarating day. Even old Sprot, the flats' caretaker, was whistling to himself as he shuffled about the yard. He hated all children and regarded them as natural nuisances. He would have liked to let the flats to no one but old age pensioners and spinster ladies.

Ally and Len ran across the Common. The tired old London trees were glistening, and there were icicles on the Temperance fountain. Alas, the park keepers must have got up very early to break the ice into lumps that looked like yellow candy. Small boys were already throwing the lumps at each other.

180   Yes, it was just the day for a foreign Count in an astrakhan collar to drive up and announce that Ally was really a foreign princess in disguise who had been dumped on the doorstep of 49 Magnolia Buildings as a baby, and that he was taking her off to reign over Ruritania where there had just been a revolution, and they were longing to welcome back their long lost

queen. All Ally's ideas about the world beyond the Common she had gleaned from the pictures or T.V. because she had never been anywhere else.

190 "Oh come on, Len," she scolded now, because all small boys are awful to walk with. Either he went round and round under her feet like a puppy on a cord, or he lagged behind and got stuck at crossings.

There was a long queue outside the cinema. When the doors were opened, the children rushed in, shouting with excitement. Ally had bought some sweets to suck, in case it was a dull film. But after a while, she did get interested in the picture. There was one girl who really had glamour in spite of her old-fashioned clothes. Lucky thing! What a time she had! Held up in stage coaches, carried off on horseback, tied to railway

200 tracks, dumped, gagged, in mines. And never a hair out of place, and a dress cut so low you'd think she must die of pneumonia.

"I've got to have glamour," Ally said to herself. On the way to the pictures, she had caught sight of her own reflection in a shop window. Her pony tail of curls of which she was usually proud had looked – well, tatty. She had grown out of her coat, and her jeans seemed odd beneath it. She had a hole in her socks and her shoes were trodden crooked. They looked awful because she had not stopped to polish them that morn-

210 ing.

When the lights went up at the end of the film, she glanced at her hands. The nails were none too clean, one was broken and the cuticles were overgrown.

You need a bathroom to look smart, she said to herself. Nothing gets the dirt off like a proper long soak.

As the heroine was clasped to the hero's breast at last, Ally made her New Year's resolution. She was going to attain glamour, even if it killed her.

ELIZABETH STUCLEY
Magnolia Buildings

A. Comprehension and Deduction

1 What exactly do you learn about living conditions at Magnolia Buildings from this passage?

2 Quite apart from the fact that it is New Year's Day, what other evidence is there in the passage that the season is winter?

3 (a) What does Ally's Mum do for a living?
(b) What do we learn from the passage about her father's employment?

4 (a) Why did Ally despair of ever achieving glamour when she went to call her brothers?
(b) Why is the morning routine in the kitchen compared with a jigsaw puzzle?

5 Sum up in your own words Mum's feelings about the way her home was run.

6 (a) Why were Ally's trousers so conspicuous to her Mum?
(b) Although Mum mocked Ally she revealed at the same time a similar interest of her childhood days. What was it?

7 Why was Mum a little worried that Val was not going to the cinema?

8 (a) What does the discussion about going to the cinema reveal of the differences in tastes for films between Ally and Len?
(b) How do you account for these differences?

9 What were the reasons for Doreen not going to the cinema?

10 From the evidence in the passage, what would you say were Mum's chief motives for working?

11 Do you find any evidence of jealousy or disapproval in Ally's feelings for Doreen? If so, give examples and explain why this should be so.

12 (a) Why did Ally eventually become interested in the film?
(b) Prior to this what had made her think seriously about her own appearance?

B. Interpretation and Criticism

1 What do you consider to be Ally's motives for wanting a room to herself?

ALLY'S NEW YEAR RESOLUTION

2 What do you learn of Ally's character and ideals from this passage? To what extent do you consider her attitude typical of a fourteen-year-old girl?

3 In what ways are Ally's views influenced by her home circumstances and social surroundings? Try to explain why.

4 (a) Why, do you think, would possessing and writing a diary have a special attraction for Ally?
(b) What would be your own reasons for keeping a diary?

5 Why are the circumstances described in this passage so ripe for Ally to become engrossed by the idea of becoming glamorous? (Consider this in detail.)

6 In what ways does the writer build up our sympathy for insignificant Auntie Glad?

7 How does the writer convey to us the predominance of Mum and the insignificance of Dad in this household?

8 In what ways do the two film titles mentioned sum up neatly the differing tastes and the boy versus girl outlooks of Len and Ally?

9 (a) In what ways is it obvious that the girls tend to be less indulged and shoulder more responsibilities than the boys in this home?
(b) Why should this be so, do you think?

10 From a consideration of (a) Ally's daydreams of a foreign count and (b) the plot of the film she saw, try to explain why films and daydreams of that nature appealed to Ally in the circumstances.

11 Write a short defence of daydreaming and romantic films.

12 (a) Do you consider this passage interesting? Give your reasons in detail.
(b) Do you consider this passage true to life? Give your reasons in detail.
(d) Do you sympathise with Ally's situation? What would be your long term solution of her problem?

C. Comment and Discussion

1 Compare this passage with The Fight (No. 11, page 56).

Both have a "local" setting. In what ways do their styles of writing differ?

2 Compare the more detailed study of the various characters in this passage with the more personal, private, self-analysis in The Fight. Why is it, therefore, more suitable for The Fight to be written in the first person and this passage in the third person?

3 Consider again question 3 of the section "Comment and Discussion" concerning the passage The Fight. Does *this* passage possess more than a merely local interest? Why?

4 Re-read Going to the Fair and question 6 of the section "Comment and Discussion" (No. 8, page 38). What have these two passages in common?

5 If the *traditional* school story does not approximate to life in the type of school many of us know, why does it retain its popularity?

14 Mercury

It was Sunday, and very hot. The holiday-makers flocked to
the hill of Mercury, to rise two thousand feet above the steamy
haze of the valleys. For the summer had been very wet, and the
heat covered the land in hot steam.

Every time it made the ascent, the funicular was crowded.
It hauled itself up the steep incline, that towards the top
looked almost perpendicular, the steel thread of the rails in the
gulf of pine-trees hanging like an iron rope against a wall.
The women held their breath, and didn't look. Or they looked
back towards the sinking levels of the river, steamed and dim,
far-stretching over the frontier.

When you arrived at the top there was nothing to do. The
hill was a pine-covered cone; paths wound between the high
tree-trunks, and you could walk round and see the glimpses of
the world all round, all round: the dim, far river-plain, with
a dull glint of the great stream, to westwards; southwards, the
black, forest-covered, agile-looking hills, with emerald-green
clearings and a white house or two; east, the inner valley, with
two villages, factory chimneys, pointed churches and hills
beyond; and north, the steep hills of forest, with reddish crags
and reddish castle ruins. The hot sun burned overhead, and
all was in steam.

Only on the very summit of the hill there was a tower, an
outlook tower; a long restaurant with its beer-garden, all the
little yellow tables standing their round disks under the horse-
chestnut trees; then a bit of rock-garden on the slope. But the
great trees began again in wilderness a few yards off.

The Sunday crowd came up in waves from the funicular.
In waves they ebbed through the beer-garden. But not many
sat down to drink. Nobody was spending any money. Some
paid to go up the outlook tower, to look down on a world of
vapours and black, agile-crouching hills, and half-crooked

towns. Then everybody dispersed along the paths, to sit among the trees in the cool air.

There was not a breath of wind. Lying and looking upwards at the shaggy, barbaric middle-world of the pine-trees, it was difficult to decide whether the pure high trunks supported the upper thicket of darkness, or whether they descended from it like great cords stretched downwards. Anyhow, in between the
40   tree-top world and the earth-world went the wonderful clean cords of innumerable proud tree-trunks, clear as rain. And as you watched, you saw that the upper world was faintly moving, faintly, most faintly swaying, with a circular movement, though the lower trunks were utterly motionless and monolithic.

There was nothing to do. In all the world, there was nothing to do, and nothing to be done. Why have we all come to the top of the Merkur? There is nothing for us to do.

What matter? We have come a stride beyond the world.
50   Let it steam and cook its half-baked reality below there. On the hill of Mercury we take no notice. Even we do not trouble to wander and pick the fat, blue, sourish bilberries. Just lie and see the rain-pure tree-trunks like chords of music between two worlds.

The hours pass by: people wander and disappear and reappear. All is hot and quiet. Humanity is rarely boisterous any more. You go for a drink: finches run among the few people at the tables: everybody glances at everybody, but with remoteness.

60   There is nothing to do but to return and lie down under the pine trees. Nothing to do. But why do anything, anyhow? The desire to do anything has gone. The tree-trunks, living like rain, they are quite active enough.

At the foot of the obsolete tower there is an old tablet-stone with a very much battered Mercury, in relief. There is also an altar, or votive stone, both from the Roman times. The Romans are supposed to have worshipped Mercury on the summit. The battered god, with his round sun-head, looks very hollow-eyed and unimpressive in the purplish-red sandstone of the district.
70   And no one any more will throw grains of offering in the

hollow of the votive stone: also common, purplish-red sandstone, very local and un-Roman.

The Sunday people do not even look. Why should they?
They keep passing on into the pine-trees. And many sit on
the benches; many lie upon the long chairs. It is very hot, in
the afternoon, and very still.

Till there seems a faint whistling in the tops of the pine-
trees, and out of the universal semi-consciousness of the afternoon arouses a bristling uneasiness. The crowd is astir, look-
80 ing at the sky. And sure enough, there is a great flat blackness
reared up in the western sky, curled with white wisps and loose
breast-feathers. It looks very sinister, as only the elements still
can look. Under the sudden weird whistling of the upper pine-
trees, there is a subdued babble and calling of frightened voices.

They want to get down; the crowd want to get off the hill
of Mercury, before the storm comes. At any price to get off
the hill! They stream towards the funicular, while the sky
blackens with incredible rapidity. And as the crowd presses
down towards the little station, the first blaze of lightning
90 opens out, followed immediately by a crash of thunder, and
great darkness. In one strange movement, the crowd takes
refuge in the deep veranda of the restaurant, pressing among
the little tables in silence. There is no rain, and no definite
wind, only a sudden coldness which makes the crowd press
closer.

They press closer, in the darkness and the suspense. They
have become curiously unified, the crowd, as if they had fused
into one body. As the air sends a chill waft under the veranda
the voices murmur plaintively, like birds under leaves, the
100 bodies press closer together, seeking shelter in contact.

The gloom, dark as night, seems to continue a long time.
Then suddenly the lightning dances white on the floor, dances
and shakes upon the ground, up and down, and lights up the
white striding of a man, lights him up only to the hips, white
and naked and striding, with fire on his heels. He seems to be
hurrying, this fiery man whose upper half is invisible, and at
his naked heels white little flames seem to flutter. His flat,
powerful thighs, his legs white as fire stride rapidly across the

open, in front of the veranda, dragging little white flames at
110 the ankles, with the movement. He is going somewhere, swiftly.

In the great bang of the thunder the apparition disappears.
The earth moves, and the house jumps in complete darkness.
A faint whimpering of terror comes from the crowd, as the
cold air swirls in. But still, upon the darkness, there is no
rain. There is no relief: a long wait.

Brilliant and blinding, the lightning falls again; a strange
bruising thud comes from the forest, as all the little tables and
secret tree-trunks stand for one unnatural second exposed. Then
the blow of the thunder, under which the house and the crowd
120 reel as under an explosion. The storm is playing directly upon
the Merkur. A belated sound of tearing branches comes out
of the forest.

And again the white splash of the lightning on the ground:
but nothing moves. And again the long, rattling, instantaneous
volleying of the thunder, in the darkness. The crowd is pant-
ing with fear, as the lightning again strikes white, and something again seems to burst, in the forest, as the thunder crashes.

At last, into the motionlessness of the storm, in rushes the
wind, with the fiery flying of bits of ice, and the sudden sea-
130 like roaring of the pine trees. The crowd winces and draws
back, as the bits of ice hit in the faces like fire. The roar of the
trees is so great, it becomes like another silence. And through
it is heard the crashing and splintering of timber, as the hurri-
cane concentrates upon the hill.

Down comes the hail, in a roar that covers every other sound,
threshing ponderously upon the ground and the roofs and the
trees. And as the crowd surges irresistibly into the interior of
the building, from the crushing of this ice-fall, still amid the
sombre hoarseness sounds the tinkle and crackle of things
140 breaking.

After an eternity of dread, it ends suddenly. Outside is a
faint gleam of yellow light, over the snow and the endless
debris of twigs and things broken. It is very cold, with the
atmosphere of ice and deep water. The forest looks wan, above
the white earth, where the ice-balls lie in their myriads, six

inches deep, littered with all the twigs and things they have broken.

"Yes! Yes!" said the men, taking sudden courage as the yellow light comes into the air. "Now we can go!"

150 The first brave ones emerge, picking up the big hailstones, pointing to the overthrown tables. Some, however, do not linger. They hurry to the funicular station, to see if the apparatus is still working.

The funicular station is on the north side of the hill. The men come back, saying there is no one there. The crowd begins to emerge upon the wet, crunching whiteness of the hail, spreading around in curiosity, waiting for the men who operate the funicular.

On the south side of the outlook tower two bodies lay in
160 the cold but thawing hail. The dark-blue of the uniforms showed blackish. Both men were dead. But the lightning had completely removed the clothing from the legs of one man, so that he was naked from the hips down. There he lay, his face sideways on the snow, and two drops of blood running from his nose into his big, blond, military moustache. He lay there near the votive stone of the Mercury. His companion, a young man, lay face downwards, a few yards behind him.

The sun began to emerge. The crowd gazed in dread, afraid to touch the bodies of the men. Why had they, the dead
170 funicular men, come round to this side of the hill, anyhow?

The funicular would not work. Something had happened to it in the storm. The crowd began to wind down the bare hill, on the sloppy ice. Everywhere the earth bristled with broken pine boughs and twigs. But the bushes and the leafy trees were stripped absolutely bare, to a miracle. The lower earth was leafless and naked as in winter.

"Absolute winter!" murmured the crowd, as they hurried, frightened, down the steep, winding descent, extricating themselves from the fallen pine-branches.
180 Meanwhile the sun began to steam in great heat.

D. H. LAWRENCE
Selected Essays

83

A. *Comprehension and Deduction*

1 For what reason did most people probably travel to the top of the hill of Mercury on this occasion?

2 Summarise the ways in which the crowds occupied their time once they reached the summit?

3 In your own words describe the kind of weather conditions prevailing when Lawrence visited the hill of Mercury.

4 What are the main features of the summit and the land just below and surrounding the summit?

5 What is the reaction of the visitors to the altar stone built for the worship of Mercury, before the storm?

6 How can the crowd hear and see that a storm is approaching?

7 (*a*) What is the first action taken by the crowd when they realise the storm is approaching?
(*b*) What action do they take when the thunder and lightning commence?

8 How does the attitude of individuals to the crowd change once the storm has begun?

9 How does Lawrence convey the impression that the apparition seen by the crowd may be the god Mercury?

10 What action does the crowd take once the hail has started to descend?

11 Compare briefly the atmosphere and the appearance of the landscape before and after the storm.

12 When exactly does the crowd begin to make a move?

13 How did it appear that the two funicular attendants had met their deaths?

14 If one considers this description carefully, it seems that the two men met their deaths for a far more terrifying reason. Bearing in mind the location of the bodies and the apparition try to construct this new interpretation of their deaths – the interpretation which Lawrence wishes us to arrive at.

15 Having made this interpretation, what would you consider to have been the supernatural purpose of the storm?

16 Is there any significance in the fact that it was the funicular drivers who met their deaths?

B   Interpretation and Criticism

1 Give a clear definition of a "funicular". (line 5)
2 What are the implications of the repetition of the word "steam" in the early paragraphs of this description?
3 What does the word "agile" suggest about the shapes of the hills in the two quotations "agile-looking hills" (line 17) and "agile-crouching hills"? (line 32)
4 Explain the meaning of the metaphor in "In waves they ebbed through the beer garden". (line 29) Why is it effective in its use here?
5 Is there any significance do you think in the constant repetition of the comment "There was nothing to do"? Why? How does the repetition fit in with the general atmosphere of the place and the people before the storm arrives? Do you see any other reason for the repetition after reconsidering the climax of this passage?
6 Can you explain why Lawrence uses the simile "like chords of music between two worlds" (lines 53-54) to describe the view of the tree trunks between the summit and the valley below?
7 Why is the crowd's uneasiness before the storm described as "bristling"? (line 79) Try to explain this in the light of the association of "bristling" with fear.
8 What does Lawrence mean when he says "They have become curiously unified, the crowd . . ."? (line 97)
9 What is the real significance of the repetition of the word "white" in the description of the apparition? (lines 102 to 110)
10 What is the effect of the apparition only being lit up to the hips, i.e. what emphasis does this give?
11 Which details in the description of the storm particularly suggest that it strips the crowd of moral fibre and virtually reduces them to the status of babies or non-human creatures.
12 What is the particular significance, in this description, of the use of the word "white" to describe the lightning?
13 What is the meaning of the word "volleying", (line 125),

used to describe the thunder and what normal association of the word makes a useful comparison here?

14 Explain the meaning of the words "surges irresistibly" in the statement "The crowd surges irresistibly into the interior of the building". (lines 137-138) What connection is there between these words and the earlier words "They ebbed through the beer garden"? (line 29) Is there any significance in the use of the stronger word "surges" at this later point in the description?

15 What is the connection in appearance between one of the dead men and the apparition?

16 How does this connection make the supernatural aspect of this study appear more credible?

C. Comment and Discussion

1 This description virtually exists on two levels. Superficially it describes an electric storm on a hill top breaking up a day of intense heat and causing the tragic death of two men. We have already discovered the supernatural story underlying this. Look again at the details in the description and consider how carefully they are selected to be symbolic of the movement of events towards the final supernatural climax.

2 Richard Aldington groups a number of Lawrence's travel essays, including this one, under the heading "The Spirit of Place". Try to discuss the methods by which Lawrence manages to endow a description of a place with a spirit which raises it above merely beautiful description of a natural scene. (Consider also, in this respect, his poem "Snake".)

15 Memories

He is a boy of eleven going to the paper-shop for his Saturday magazine, for the *Wizard* or the *Hotspur*. Here he passes a shop where they never grumble at being asked to sell pennyworths of sweets, here a pal's father smoking in the doorway in his shirtsleeves, after the last shift before the week-end: here a broken-down wooden fence out of which large spiders can be teased: here the off-licence with its bell clanging as someone comes out with a small jug of vinegar.

There are the varieties of light he will know: the sun forc-
10 ing its way down as far as the ground-floor windows on a very sunny afternoon, the foggy grey of November over the slates and chimneys, the misty evenings of March when the gangs congregate in the watery yellow light of the kicked and scratched gas-lamp. Or the smells: the beer-and-Woodbine smell of the men on Saturday nights, the cheap powder-and-cream smell of his grown-up sisters, fish-and-chips, the fresh starchiness of new clothes at Whitsun, the pervasive aura of urine – dog, cat and human. Most attractive of all, a scene with noise, light and smell – between eleven and twelve on a sunny
20 Saturday morning, when all doors are open and most steps occupied; the roast beef gives out its flavour from almost every house, the wirelesses mix their noises with each other, you can hear families talking or laughing or quarrelling. But there is little quarrelling just now; over almost all is a sense of ease, recreation and good food to come.

A few years ago he would have known the "tingle-airyes" (barrel-organs or street-pianos); they were hired by the day from a depot in town by seedy old men, and provided working-class housewives with their morning music before the wireless
30 made the Light Programme and Radio Luxembourg available. They had a flighty and apparently uncertain manner of play-ing, all runs and cascades inside a regular series of great swings of melody; every tune was translated into an affair of burplings

and flutings, of trollopy flirtings and gurgly runs, with a particularly skittish twirl at the end of each movement. If I hear "Valencia" or "I Left My Heart in Avalon" nowadays, no matter how played, I hear it poignantly as the street-pianos played it. They have gone, but little hand-operated round-abouts on carts still come round, announced by a great clang-40 ing bell; and the rag-and-bone men still shout out offers of goldfish for old clothes and jam-jars.

There are the boy's odder pleasures of taste, not so much the ordinary toffees and boiled sweets, nor even the sherbet-fountains, monkey nuts and aniseed balls, but the stuff of which each generation of boys transmits the secret – a penny stick of licorice or some cinnamon root from the chemist, two pennyworth of broken locust, a portion of chips "with some scraps, please", well soused with salt and vinegar and eaten out of a piece of newspaper which is licked at the end. Eaten 50 in this way, as you slowly walk down the pavement at night, they are delicious.

There is the animal life of the neighbourhood: the crowd of domestic pets, with mongrel dogs the most interesting, though cats are more numerous than dogs. The starlings occupy the public buildings in town, but sparrows abound here and occasional pigeons raid the cobblestones; mice can be found in the communal middens, and ladybirds have a way of appearing in the mucky bits of back-garden; at the end of the yard may be an orange-box for a few rabbits or an elaborately tiered 60 series of crates housing budgerigars.

There are the occasional special excitements – a funeral or a wedding in the street, a chimney on fire, a coalman's horse down on the icy cobbles, an attempted gassing in the kitchen oven, a family row which can be heard from half a dozen doors away on each side. Most absorbing of all to a boy are the games of the street, with the lamp-post taking the place of the tree on a village green. Between five and thirteen, roughly, you play with your own sex. Games change as the year unfolds, following the products of the season (e.g. "conkers"), or simply 70 by the boys' own intuitively followed rhythm. At one time everyone is playing "taws", with his marbles ranked in prestige

according to age and killing power; quite suddenly marbles
go out and everybody wants a threepenny peashooter. Occasionally new amusements have a vogue, like the yo-yo of the
'thirties, but usually these are only temporary. Games should
normally require no equipment other than a ball or stick;
they should make use of available materials, of the lamp-posts,
the flagstones and the flat ends of houses. Hoops and shuttle-
cocks have almost entirely gone, and whips-and-tops are not so
80 popular now; but "piseball", "tig", hopscotch across the flags
and a great number of games involving running round the
lamp-posts or in and out of the closet-areas, such as "Cowboys
and Indians", are still popular. Girls still like skipping-ropes,
and almost peculiar to them is the game of dressing-up – trail-
ing round the streets in grown-ups' cast-off clothes and old lace,
as "a wedding". Now and again a couple of boys set to work
in a back-yard and make a "bogey" out of a couple of planks
and the wheels off an old pram: then they race down the pavements or on the nearest bit of tarmac'd road, operating the
90 wooden hand-brake as they approach the tram-route.

    Rhyming chants survive, to accompany the games – "eeny-
meeny-miny-mo"; "one-two-three-a'lairy": "tinker-tailor-sol-
dier-sailor": "I like coffee, I like tea. I like sitting on a black
man's knee". For the rest, there are songs on only a few occasions – the voting song, "Vote, Vote, Vote for Mister . . ." an
occasional Bonfire Night collecting song; and the chants used,
in a flat sing-song, after a few carols at a house-door:

> Christmas is coming; the goose is getting fat,
> Please put a penny in the old man's hat.
100 If you haven't got a penny a ha'penny will do,
> If you haven't got a ha'penny – God bless you.

or

> We wish you a merry Christmas; we wish you a merry Christ-
> mas;
> We wish you a merry Christmas, and a Happy New Year.

    Of "outings", those recreations which involve spending a

few coppers or leaving the home-ground, the sequence is determined almost entirely by the seasons. There are outings with
jam-jars to a dirty stream a mile or so away, for sticklebacks
110 and red-throats; blackberrying, also with jam-jars, even
farther afield, past the church with the whalebone arches; raids
on the nearest rhubarb and turnip fields, or a little birds'-
nesting. Those who can cadge a few coppers from their mothers
go to the public baths; or occasionally catch a tram to some
remote part of the city where the children's playground is said
to be good, and spend the whole day there with a few sand-
wiches and a bottle of pop between the lot of them. In autumn,
whole days can be passed watching the "feast" set up, and
working out what it will be possible to go on.
120 So the days and the weeks succeed one another, often dull
and grey, but relieved by all kinds of excitements. There is a
rhythm, but it is the rhythm of a brick-world, to which those
of the seasons or of the great religious festivals are only incidental. At each week-end, perhaps, there is Friday night's shopping with Mother down a shopping street that is all bustle and
warmth and gregarious spending, and the trams rattle and
flash past constantly. There is the whole week-end ahead, with
the pictures on Saturday, or a chapel concert with a hot supper
in the Sunday school room; bacon and eggs for Sunday break-
130 fast, the big Sunday tea. Then, throughout the year, Pancake
Tuesday, Voting Day, which is always a holiday, Hotcross
Buns on Good Friday, the Autumn "Feast", Mischief Night,
and all the weeks of cadging and collecting for Bonfire Night.
It is a truly urban fire, with very little wood that has known
a tree for the last few years, a fire composed of old mattresses
and chairs – replaced now that someone's club turn has come
up – or a horsehair sofa displaced by a modern one on hire
purchase. As the fireworks run out, you bake potatoes round
the fire's edges.

RICHARD HOGGART
The Uses of Literacy

A. Comprehension and Deduction

1 Three words, all mentioned in paragraph 2, sum up what paragraph 2 is about. Write down these words.

2 What would appear to be the chief occupations of the men of the neighbourhood on Saturday mornings?

3 Where would the groups of youths be likely to meet in the evenings, and why would they choose this spot do you think?

4 (a) Which Sunday meal-time delicacies mentioned here suggest by their very mentioning, that meals during the week are less nourishing?
(b) Why should this be so?

5 How were the latest "pop" tunes introduced to this neighbourhood before the days of radio and television?

6 What kind of road surface was most commonly used in this neighbourhood? Describe how the surface is laid, briefly.

7 What uses were made of various parts of the neighbourhood for games?

8 Why was it necessary to find "pavements" or "the nearest bit of tarmac'd road" to race "bogeys"?

9 Explain the difference in use between the rhyming chants and the occasional rhymes used in the neighbourhood.

10 What was the difference between an "outing" and, say, a race with "bogeys" down the street?

B. Interpretation and Criticism

1 Look at the words describing the smells of men, grown up sisters and clothes in paragraph 2. What do you learn about the neighbourhood from these descriptions? Explain why these particular descriptions help you to reach your conclusions.

2 Try to explain the exact meaning of the words "pervasive aura". (line 17)

3 (a) Why should barrel-organs be known by the nickname of "tingle-airyes"? (line 26)
(b) Why were they popular?

(c) Try to sum up, in your own words, the style of musical arrangement found in barrel organ tunes. Why were they arranged in such styles?

4 What does the writer mean by the phrase, "the stuff of which each generation of boys transmits the secret"? (lines 44-45)

5 What were the "scraps" asked for with a portion of chips? (line 48)

6 Why would most dogs in this neighbourhood be mongrel dogs?

7 Explain the appearance of "an elaborately tiered series of crates". (lines 59-60)

8 Try to explain, using your own pattern of games if you wish, what the writer means when he refers to "the boys' own intuitively followed rhythm" of games. (line 70)

9 What is the meaning of the word "vogue" in the statement: "occasionally new amusements have a vogue"? (line 74)

10 Why should Friday night be a shopping night with Mother?

11 Why does the writer call the bonfire "a truly urban fire"? (line 134)

12 Write down the subject headings which would help to form the basis of a summary of this passage.

C. Comment and Discussion

This description of the typical features of a working-class area, as they appear to a working-class boy now, and a few years ago, was written by Richard Hoggart and forms part of a lengthy, extremely readable study of sociology entitled *The Uses of Literacy*. It deals with the same type of neighbourhood as that represented in the passage The Fight (No. 11, page 56). Both authors spent their childhood in the same city, Leeds, and the two passages are worth looking at in conjunction.

The following questions are worth considering:

1 Which details in this passage suggest that the author is writing from first-hand experience in his own childhood rather than from the results of later research?

2 How does the writer make what could be a very a ademic piece of social study a most attractive and readable piece of description?

3 To what extent does your reading of this passage add to your understanding and appreciation of the social background of the passage entitled The Fight, and vice-versa?

16 Steam's Last Mileposts

"You see something for your work on a steam engine," said fireman Alec Mackay as he prepared to shovel three tons of coal between York and Edinburgh. "You go home tired from a diesel."

Alec Mackay is an unshakable devotee of steam engines, like so many other railwaymen. But steam is fast disappearing from British Railways, and on Friday another chapter in railway history came to an end when the Elizabethan express pulled into Waverley station, Edinburgh.

10 It was the last run of the world's longest and fastest non-stop steam-hauled express – 392½ miles from King's Cross to Edinburgh in 395 minutes. Soon the diesels will have taken over the East Coast route, rapidly becoming one of the most modernised sections of British Railways.

Appropriately the Elizabethan was hauled for the last run by *Mallard*, holder of the world speed record for steam of 126 miles an hour, and designed by the late Sir Nigel Gresley, the last of the long line of great British railway engineers that began with George Stephenson and *Locomotion* at Darlington.

20 For many people British Railways are unfortunately personified by the unhelpful porter on a city station. But what of the operating railwaymen, on the footplate, in the lonely signal box, or maintaining the track, the men who keep the wheels turning night and day to carry over 1,000 m. people a year in almost total safety?

They are none-too-well paid; a driver may average £17 a week over the year, a fireman £13, though top men can make more. But almost all in my experience are men with a pride in the job too rarely found elsewhere today. Railway work – sig-
30 nificantly, the men always refer to the "Service" – calls for steadiness, reliability and integrity of character. It is no coincidence that the railwaymen of France provided the most trustworthy element in the Resistance during the war, or that the months-long strike of Dutch railwaymen was one of the

94

greatest collective acts of defiance of the Germans.

Travelling to Edinburgh in *Mallard*'s cab, I saw something of British railwaymen and their work. Our two crews – a corridor through the tender allows them to change over without stopping – were as typical as you could find.

40 From London to York the driver was Harold Birkett, a quiet, unshakable man with 47 years' service behind him, yet still basically a countryman, and his fireman John Thorne. At 22, Thorne is unusually young to be working a crack express. He is passionately interested in railways; modernisation made him redundant at Nottingham, but he moved to London rather than leave the service.

At York Alec Mackay and driver Bob Currie came on to the footplate. Currie, who began as a train register boy in 1913, shared his fireman's enthusiasm for steam. " It's a real pleasure 50 to step on to an engine in good form like this one," he told me.

Their two London colleagues preferred diesels. " But," said Driver Birkett, " it's not so easy when you're turned 60 to go back to school and learn about electricity, wiring and all the other details."

There are other snags too. " You can always keep a steam engine going and you can always get a bit more out of it. But when a diesel stops, it stops."

It is the steam engine that is the more sensitive machine, and part of the satisfaction of driving one lies in its responsive-60 ness to the crew's skill. A computer can calculate the performance and timing of a diesel engine; its maximum load and speed is pre-ordained. The machine is master. The diesel driver merely releases the power already there. Steam is a craft, the crew jointly creating and utilising power.

" No two drivers are alike," said Mackay, " a fireman can soon tell the difference between a driver and a hash. . . ." " And a good fireman knows just when his driver needs that little bit more steam," added Currie.

I saw the partnership between crew and machine at close 70 quarters in the cab of *Mallard*. From the moment when Birkett opened the regulator at King's Cross there was unceasing activity on the footplate. A footplate rocking and vibrating, heat blazing from the firebox, one's ears deafened by a continual roar broken every few minutes by the automatic warning system – a bell as we approached a signal at green, a siren for caution.

For the fireman it is an endless round of stoking, adjusting the injector to keep the right water level in the boiler (*Mallard* consumed 40 pounds of coal and 35 gallons of water a mile),
80 and watching for signals on the driver's blind side. Between shovelfuls there is the footplate. to be hosed and swept to keep the dust down. Six times between London and Edinburgh we dropped the scoop to pick up water.

For the driver it is a matter of unceasing vigilance for signals, speed restrictions and timekeeping – supplemented nowadays by the automatic warning system. This vigilance, the signalmen checking the train past en route and the gangers inspecting the track, all combine to give a striking sense of security, even in the rocking cab.
90 There's an 11-mile climb out of King's Cross, and Harry Birkett took it quietly, conserving his steam. We had left two minutes late, but it was not until Potter's Bar that we touched 60 and began making it up. Hitchin, 32 miles, was passed at 80 and on time.

But soon after we had the first check – caused by modernisation work, a long stretch at 20 m.p.h. over relaid track, which set us back 3½ minutes. Then there was the slow crawl through the sharp curves at Peterborough and the hard climb up to Stoke Summit, the highest point on the line. But in between
100 Harold Birkett had our 359-ton load of 10 coaches travelling for long periods at up to 88 m.p.h. York was passed at 12.37, three minutes early.

Neither of our drivers used a watch much or relied on the speedometer. The speedometer has only recently been fitted, and for some reason deep in history watches are issued only to guards.

Most drivers have an instinctive knowledge of the speeds required by the timetable. Likewise their bump of locality is either instinct or something that's meaningless to the traveller;
110 the feel of the line, the sound of a bridge or tunnel. Station

names aren't much use in the middle of a stormy night.

At York we entered the heart of modern railwayland, where the signalmen control trains they don't even see; then on to Darlington, the railways' birthplace; Newcastle, home of George Stephenson's original locomotive works and of his son Robert's cast-iron high-level bridge over the Tyne, and so to the magnificent sweep of the Royal Border Bridge, also by Robert.

120 As we came in sight of Edinburgh Castle and Bob Currie closed his regulator and gently applied the brakes, I wondered whether all this was just a sentimental reverie. Great men, great engines, great records – all of the past. What of the future, with air and road transport expanding so rapidly?

Across the English Channel the French have no doubts. French Railways, given high priority in modernisation under the Monet plan, are booming with the rest of the nation and leading the world in speed and technical development.

My companions had no doubts either. " In a few years' time it will be a great job," said Mackay. Chief Motive Power
130 Inspector Bert Dixon, who travelled with us, told me that improved wages and the chance of working on a modernised system were already attracting a better type of young entrant although wages, many may think, have still a long way to go to be a just reward.

The next few months will see 22 English Electric 3,300 horsepower diesels replace 55 steam locomotives on the East Coast main line (the diesel can work 22 hours out of 24, compared with steam's eight hours). The Deltics are the world's most powerful single-unit diesel engines. Their rapid acceleration
140 and powerful braking will allow faster timings than is possible with steam. Leeds in three hours, Newcastle in four and Edinburgh in six is the target, a level reached only by the short and specially-built Coronation and Silver Jubilee trains.

Steam may have its charms, but it could never achieve this as a regular service with a standard train. The next few years may well see a second railway revolution.

IAN WALLER
The Sunday Telegraph

97

A. Comprehension and Deduction

1 Why did Ian Waller make a footplate trip on this occasion?
2 Why did British Railways probably select *Mallard* as the engine for this trip?
3 What proof is there of Fireman Thorne's real enthusiasm for railway work?
4 Why did Driver Birkett probably prefer steam locomotives to diesel locomotives?
5 Explain in your own words the basic difference between driving a diesel locomotive and driving a steam locomotive.
6 What other duties did the fireman appear to perform beside stoking the fire?
7 Why did Driver Birkett not make up the two minutes lost time until after Potter's Bar?
8 What were the two reasons for speed reduction at certain points on this journey, prior to braking at the end of the run?
9 (*a*) Which instruments are surprisingly little used on the footplate?
(*b*) Why and how can the driver largely dispense with them?
10 Where, and how, did the change of engine crew take place? Why was this point probably chosen?
11 Why, according to the facts given here, would it be possible to run speedier expresses on this route when diesels replaced steam locomotives?
12 From the information given, sum up the advantages and disadvantages of both steam and diesel locomotives.

B. Interpretation and Criticism

1 Explain exactly what the writer means when he says that Alec Mackay is "an unshakable devotee of steam engines" (line 5)
2 When the writer states that "For many people British Railways are unfortunately personified by the unhelpful porter on a city station" what exactly does he mean by the word "personified"? (lines 20-21)

3 (a) What is "integrity of character"? (line 31)
   (b) Why is it particularly necessary for a railwayman to possess this quality?

4 (a) What is a "collective act"? (line 35)
   (b) Give examples of "collective acts" typical of the world today.
   (c) What is "collective security" when applied to international affairs?

5 (a) What does the writer mean by saying "Modernisation made him redundant at Nottingham"? (lines 44-45)
   (b) Try to give another example of redundancy caused by modernisation.

6 What does the writer mean when he refers to the steam engine as "the more *sensitive* machine"? (line 58)

7 (a) What is a "craft" (line 58) in its general sense?
   (b) Why, therefore, does the writer say that "steam is a craft"? (line 63)

8 Which word, used in the passage, sums up the quality of watchfulness found in all key railway workers?

9 What is the meaning of the phrase "their bump of locality"? (line 108)

10 Try to explain the circumstances under which the signalmen at York "control trains they don't even see". (line 113)

11 (a) What is "motive power"? (line 129)
   (b) What supplied "motive power" on this trip?
   (c) What, therefore, would Bert Dixon's duties as Inspector probably involve?

12 Bearing in mind the comment made by the writer concerning the Coronation and Silver Jubilee trains, how would you define "a standard train"? (line 145)

13 Why does the writer write rather regretfully on this occasion, even though the new diesels will improve railway services?

C. Comment and Discussion

1 As in the passage The Night Riders, this passage is a Feature Article written by a journalist for a national news-

paper. What is the purpose of a Feature Article in a newspaper?

2   How does the use of direct quotation add to one's interest in reading this article? (See also The Night Riders No. 10, page 50.)

3   Consider to what extent the scientific facts contained in this article will be more likely to be remembered because of the style in which the article is written and the incidental way in which facts and figures are introduced.

4   Many writers on railway topics adopt a sensational approach in their writings. Consider the possibilities for sensational writing in an article such as this and note the ways in which this writer conveys a sense of excitement without being deliberately sensational.

5   Finally, this article was written because the material was topical at the time. It is no longer topical – but it is still very readable. Why?

17 The Kidnappers

His first conscious thought was that even for a nightmare it was extraordinarily cold and uncomfortable, and the noise was incredible. The sensation of being unable to speak was more familiar to him in dreams, and he moved his throbbing head restlessly, fighting as he thought with sleep. Soon he realised that he was awake, but in such an astonishing position that he doubted his sanity.

He was wedged tightly into a little wheeled chair, midway between an invalid carriage and child's go-cart, his arms 10 pinioned to his sides under an old khaki mackintosh fastened behind him, and his cramped legs drawn up and strapped to the undercarriage of the chair. His mouth was sealed with a strip of adhesive plaster, which irritated abominably and paralysed the lower part of his face. He was wearing a knitted balaclava helmet which covered his entire head save his eyes, and he was being wheeled swiftly along a foggy gutter in the midst of a rabble of marching men, who kept time to the thin music of a mouth-organ.

At this point he remembered what had happened to him up 20 to the instant at which he had been knocked out, and he had the presence of mind not to attempt any violent movement which would have betrayed his return to consciousness. Having made certain that he really was helpless, trussed neatly by experienced hands, just able to breathe but no more, he concentrated cautiously on his kidnappers.

There were ten or a dozen of them, drab, shadowy figures who kept very close to him, shielding him with their bodies from passers-by who could scarcely see their own hands in front of their faces in the brown mist.

30 From where Geoffrey sat, very close to the ground, they towered above him, and lighted buses crawling by looked big as showboats and as remote. His head was spinning and he

was still fighting with incredulity, but by this time the shuffling ghosts nearest to him had resolved into men and he noticed with a shock that there was something odd about each of them, although for people with such emphasised disabilities they seemed to move with surprising freedom and lightness. The only heavy feet were those which stamped immediately behind his chair. The rest padded softly round him in the lamplit
40 gloom, their clothes whispering and rustling in his ear.

The man directly in front of him was leading the way. He was tall and made monstrously so by the fact that on his shoulders he carried a dwarf, a small man whose normal conveyance was no doubt the wheeled chair now occupied by the prisoner. It was the dwarf who played the mouth-organ. Geoffrey could see his small elbows moving in an ecstasy of excitement and pleasure. Geoffrey's own dark hat, punched up into a billycock, sat on the back of the little man's bulbous head, and from time to time he paused in his playing to jam
50 it more securely in position.

It was the tune which gave Geoffrey Levett the essential clue. He remembered it as a sentimental dirge of the Second World War called "Waiting". He had been hearing it at intervals all the afternoon, played execrably by an "Ex-Servicemen's" band up and down Crumb Street. This was the same band.

He made the discovery with a certain amount of relief, since it took him at least out of the region of pure fantasy and into the merely thoroughly outrageous, with which as a modern he
60 was by now more or less familiar. The group had haunted him all through his nervous vigil outside the police station, pestering him with offhand importunities. But he saw now that it must have been his own quarry, the man in the sports jacket, for whom they had been waiting. They had certainly found him, but what they had done with him he had no idea. He did not appear to be with them.

He decided that the business was doubtless some kind of minor gang warfare, and his own part in it must be entirely accidental. By some mistake he had been knocked down and
70 collected instead of the man they had called "Duds".

Doubtless they were taking him somewhere now with the idea of questioning him.

The little procession halted abruptly. It took him by surprise and jerked him forward in the chair. The mouth-organ squealed and was silent, and he was aware of nervousness all round him. One man on his left giggled stupidly.

A silver-crested helmet looked out of the fog and the voice of the law, casual and consciously superior, drawled down at them.

80 "Packing up for the night, Doll?"

"That's right, Orficer. It's a nasty night. Warmer at 'ome."

Geoffrey recognised the courage in the new voice, which came from behind him. It belonged to Heavy Boots, he decided, for he felt his carriage quiver as the hands on its rails trembled. Yet the tone was perfectly easy and ingratiating.

"You're right there." The law spoke with feeling. "What have you got there?"

Geoffrey achieved a snort through his muffler and at once an iron hand closed on his shoulder. He became aware of the

90 stink of fear reeking all round him, but Heavy Boots seemed quite equal to the occasion.

"It's only poor Blinky, Orficer." And then with dreadful confiding, "Fits. 'E 'as 'em."

"I see. Very well." The law granted his permission to the ills of man with condescension, not to say haste. "Good night, all."

He moved on with steady dignity.

"Good night, Orficer." Heavy Boots showed no signs of relief, but his voice rose warningly to cover any signs of eager-

100 ness in the others. "Get along, Tom, can't you. Strike up, 'Ercules. Blinkey ought to be in bed, Blinky did."

The procession was moving at speed, and the dwarf, after much prompting, achieved a few scattered notes on his mouth-organ. Heavy Boots swore softly for a little while. He had an ugly vocabulary and a line of suppressed savagery which was startling. Geoffrey heard "the Flattie" consigned to several sorts of perdition, some of them new to him. As an introduction, the incident was revealing. Geoffrey understood he had but one man to deal with.

110 With the danger past, the temper of the band rose noticeably, and the men on the left who giggled showed signs of hysteria until he was silenced by a kick on the shins from Heavy Boots, who scarcely paused in his stride to administer it. The dwarf was playing merrily again by the time they turned out of the dark street into a lane, which despite the fog was ablaze from end to end with light and bustle.

It was a market, Geoffrey saw, one of those small Alsatias which are still dotted about the poorer parts of the city, protected by ancient custom and the independence of their 120 patrons. Ramshackle stalls roofed with flapping tarpaulin and lit with naked bulbs jostled each other down each side of the littered road; their merchandise, which ranged from whelks to underwear, was open to the sooty air, while behind them tottering shops, open-fronted and ill lit, cowered odorously.

The band kept to the middle of the road and closed very tightly round the chair. For the first time Geoffrey was aware of their faces and he recognised some of them from seeing them in Crumb Street that afternoon. The giggling man turned out to be a hunchback, taller than most of his kind but typical, 130 with a jaw like a trowel and lank black hair which flapped as he moved. A one-armed man, his sleeve swinging mightily, strode close beside him, while a flying figure, festooned with picturesque rags and moving with amazing speed and dexterity, swung himself between a pair of crutches just in front. No one spoke to them. There were no greetings from the traders, no pleasantries. They passed by without a head being turned.

The end of the journey came suddenly. At a gap between two stalls the group swung sharply and they plunged into darkness again. This time it was through a doorway beside a 140 greengrocer's shop, partly shuttered now, but still sprouting wilted leaves and damp straw all over the pavement.

The hallway was narrow and chill and it smelt of dirt and damp and that particular stink of city poverty which is uncompromisingly cat. It was also pitch dark. But there was no delay. The procession dived like rats into a hole, and Geoffrey

and his little chair were swept on and down until an inner
door swung suddenly open and he found himself at the head
of a dimly lit flight of cellar stairs. There he stopped, held pre-
cariously on the top step while the rest swept past him,
150 bobbing and weaving down the dangerous way with the ease
of long practice.

He found he was looking into a vast shadowy cavern, warm
and smelling unexpectedly wholesome and countrified, like a
toolshed or a barn. He was struck first by its neatness. There
was order, even homeliness, in its arrangement. Its size was
enormous. It took up the whole cellar of the building. It was
very high, and although black and cobwebby as to rafters, the
walls were clean and whitewashed up to a height of ten feet
or so. A mighty iron stove, gleaming with lead and very nearly
160 red-hot, stood out in the room, and round it was a circle of
seats, junk-shop chairs and settees covered with festoons of
clean sacks. Three plank tables placed end-to-end, covered with
clean newspapers and flanked by packing-case benches, stood
waiting behind them, and far away against the farther wall a
row of couches stacked with army blankets presented neat ends
to the view.

Geoffrey recognised it at once. He had seen places like it
before, when a Company on active service under a good ser-
geant had dug itself in in some long-held position. Everywhere
170 there were signs of discipline and a particular kind of per-
sonality. No rubbish or odds-and-ends were in sight, but all
round the walls little packages of possessions, tied up in sack-
ing, were hung neatly on nails, very much as one finds them
in old-fashioned cottages or blacksmiths' shops. It was a
definite variety of bachelor establishment, in fact; primitive
and wholly masculine, yet not without a trace of civilisation.

His scrutiny was cut short in a most terrifying manner. The
men below him scattered. There was a shrill scream, wild and
ecstatic, from the dwarf, and at the same instant the hands
180 holding his chair were suddenly withdrawn, so that the little
carriage began a dreadful descent down the steep stairs, while
he was powerless to leave or guide it.

The utter brutality of the gesture, its careless savagery and recklessness, terrified him much more than the physical danger. There was nothing he could do to save himself. His weight speeded the little wheels and he hurled himself backward, his spine arched, in an attempt to prevent himself from pitching head first on to the brick floor. By something which he dimly realised was not quite a miracle, but some peculiar adroitness 190 in the method of launching, the chair did not over-balance, but it rocked wildly as it touched ground and sped through the whooping crowd, to crash into a pile of paper-filled sacks stacked against the wall. Their position was far too lucky to be accidental. Without them, the chair itself, not to mention half the bones in his body, must have been broken, and he realised even before the dwarf had ceased his delighted yelping that this must be a cruelty which had been practised on the little man himself many times, perhaps every day.

He felt deathly sick. The adhesive plaster was suffocating 200 him, and in the warm air the knitted helmet irritated unbearably. Once, to his horror, he thought he was going to faint, but the heavy feet were clattering across the bricks towards him and he made a great effort at control. The newcomer approached and bent down.

Geoffrey looked up and for the first time set eyes on his persecutor. He saw a big, shambling figure, stooped and loose-jointed, middle-aged but still very powerful. The startling thing about him was his colour. He was so white that he was shocking, his close-cropped hair so much the colour of his skin 210 that the line of demarcation was scarcely visible. Black glasses which hid his eyes explained him. He was an albino, one of those unlucky few in whom the natural pigmentation of the body is entirely absent. He was seeing his prisoner for the first time. The dim light suited his weak eyes and he swung the chair round slowly to get a better view.

MARGERY ALLINGHAM
The Tiger in the Smoke

A. Comprehension and Deduction

1   Explain clearly, and in your own words, what had apparently happened to Geoffrey.

2   (a) Who were his captors?
(b) How did he recognise them?

3   Why did he not shout out when the policeman stopped the group?

4   Why, previously, had he not attempted to move at all?

5   What was the wheeled-chair normally used for?

6   Explain in your own words why Geoffrey was rather relieved to recognise his captors.

7   Explain exactly how Geoffrey considered that he had become mixed up in this business and for what purpose he was being wheeled along through the streets.

8   (a) Who appeared to be the spokesman for the group when they were stopped by the policeman?
(b) What excuse did he give for Geoffrey's situation and appearance?
(c) Why did this incident provide Geoffrey with information which would make him feel a little more relieved?

9   How did the weather conditions and the time of day help his captors?

10 What precautions did the group take when they reached the street market?

11 (a) What struck Geoffrey most about the general appearance of the cellar?
(b) Sum up the ways in which the men and their cellar reminded Geoffrey of service life.

12 (a) What happened to Geoffrey to interrupt his thoughts when he first saw the cellar?
(b) What proof did he have that this happening was an everyday occurrence to the real occupant of the chair?

13 What other physical discomforts was Geoffrey suffering?

14 What was the most outstanding feature of Geoffrey's " persecutor "?

B. *Interpretation and Criticism*

1 (*a*) What is the implication of the opening phrase, "His first conscious thought"?
(*b*) What other evidence later makes this certain?

2 (*a*) What is a "balaclava helmet"? (line 15)
(*b*) Why did this probably suggest to Geoffrey that his captors were ex-servicemen?

3 (*a*) What is the meaning of the word "trussed" in the phrase "trussed neatly by experienced hands"? (line 23)
(*b*) What creatures are sometimes "trussed" and for what purpose?
(*c*) Why, therefore, is this word rather appropriately used here?

4 Express more simply the statement, "He was still fighting with incredulity." (line 33)

5 Why is the song "Waiting" described as "a sentimental *dirge*"? (line 52) (Consider particularly the meaning of the word "dirge".)

6 Suggest the words possibly used by the members of the band when they pestered Geoffrey "with offhand importunities" (line 62) as he waited outside the police station.

7 Why was the tone used by Heavy Boots in addressing the policeman "ingratiating"? (line 85) Why was Heavy Boots no doubt used to being ingratiating?

8 Why were the chairs in the cellar described as "junk-shop chairs"? (line 161)

9 What is the meaning of the phrase "on active service"? (line 168)

10 (*a*) What is the present civilian meaning of the phrase "dig oneself in"? (line 169)
(*b*) What was the original military meaning of this phrase?

11 Why is the word "scrutiny" used rather than the words "study" or "observation" or "survey" in the statement, "His scrutiny was cut short in a most terrifying manner"? (line 177)

12 What is meant by the phrase, "By some peculiar adroitness in the method of launching"? (lines 189-190)

13 Explain the meaning of the phrase "the line of demarcation". (line 210)

C. Comment and Discussion

A foggy night, a kidnapping, a cellar in which the gang live, a group of deformed and sinister characters. All these are good basic ingredients for thrills, but their effective mixing requires considerable skill if one is to gain pleasure from reading the story in addition to the automatic spine chillings of the situation presented. Consider Margery Allingham's skill in creating this pleasure for us here. Note the restrained style of writing. By careful attention to detail the full implication of the situation can be brought out without the need to sensationalise. Consider how a less skilful writer by sensationalising the violence would remove the actual terror. Note too the use of emotive words which create an intended feeling in the reader, (e.g. "shuffling ghosts", "shambling figure") the exact descriptions of persons and things, and the way in which even in this short extract the members of the band assume individual characteristics – they are not just an impersonal gang of kidnappers.

Compare the style of this passage, from an English thriller, with that of "Shots in the Dark" (No. 2) taken from an American thriller.

18 Journey to the Coal Face

Suddenly we are in an even lower tunnelway, dimly lit by far-spaced electric bulbs in small wire cages. The walls on both sides consist of four to five feet of stone "packing" built on each side of the road after the coal was removed. To walk is to walk stooped. I follow the sound of footsteps. After a hundred yards I find myself looking for the opening where I can straighten up again; instead, the tunnel narrows. This is the main highway for workers to get to the Sleythorpe seam, and it is necessary for us to walk doubled over completely.

10 Sweat is pouring from me. I try to watch how MacLane and Bolton do it but can detect no discernible style. It seems to me they are racing ahead, stepping skilfully and surely between the wooden ties of the narrow-gauge tracks which constantly trip me up, and every time I stumble my head jerks up and slams my skull against the roof, sending my helmet either flying or jamming it painfully down over my ears. To avoid the tracks I adopt a kind of crouching, rolling gait, wasteful motion, but it helps me keep up.

Doubled over in the hot darkness, sweating, barely able to 20 see my hand in front of my face, my ears humming with the depth (1800 feet plus what? I keep asking myself) and the ventilators and dynamo thrum, I stumble on. It seems hours since we left the luxury of the paddy train. My back is killing me, my legs are beginning to tremble, I have skinned my arms and face, and MacLane says, over his shoulder, "As you can see, this is the easiest part. We're just taking the way the ordinary miner does to get to his face. Later on, you'll see some of the work."

Sections of hard grey rock, men's faces, flashing bulbs, damp 30 blackened trousers contribute to sense reception, but nothing mixes. The single point of reference I have is the completely assured manner of my conductors, MacLane and Bolton, who, though hunched over double as I am, maintain a steady walking pace while MacLane briefs me. I grunt unintelligently from time to time and wonder how it was for them when they first went down to the mines, Bolton at 13, MacLane at 14, and how long it took for this to become their way of life.

For ten minutes, quarter of an hour, twenty minutes we walk along in this way while the air becomes closer, hotter, darker. The men we pass no longer wear their outer shirts but are down, some of them, to shorts and under-vests. I happen upon my first landmark: the smiling and brawny giant, Frank, no longer in his coloured nylon shirt sent him by a cousin in Philadelphia, but in grime-encrusted canvas shorts, bare chest and knee pads. Frank sees to it that MacLane and Bolton can't see him, and he mock-presents arms with his pick.

Now we're coming into knee-pad territory. Crack! Off spins my helmet. Bolton cannot resist turning and grinning full into my face. On and on we go. Even MacLane has to turn back and smile. I have discovered that the most efficient way, for me, to do the roadway is a sort of duck-squat, harder on the legs but easier on the back. I remember something Davie once said to me: "A face worker can spend his whole life down in pit without once straightening up to his full height." I also remember he said that at Beckley pit he had to walk one mile along planks on his hands and knees, which is virtually what we're doing now, just to get to his place of work. "But Dinlock pit," he promised, "is better."

Now, as we get down deeper and deeper, towards what must be (I am thinking) some sort of molten core, it becomes intermittently possible, in short patches, to walk upright, only to be forced to stoop down again for another hundred or two hundred yards. Bolton drops back and says, "Was a tahm, not too far back, when the men had to walk all the way from cage head. No paddy cars." Then he rejoins MacLane with whom he seems to be having some sort of reunion. They point out various things to each other. It is all I can do to see I don't fall on my face. My legs stop; I can't go any further. Something has grabbed them. I start; I tug frantically, not wanting to know what has overtaken me and not surprised, only wanting to escape its clutches. "Hello, lad! Heard tha' were coomin' down today! " It is fat Eddie Bullen, his paunch hanging pendulously over his shorts made of old trousers scissored down. He is guarding a small dynamo. Eddie isn't a face worker and so it is easy to recognise him. "Ah told tha' Ah had an easy job," he says. Right here the air is like a thick gas whistling past us in gusts. I say hello to Eddie, and we give each other the thumbs-up sign.

80 And stumble on, keeping my eyes strained to the floor of the roadway, one hand latched around the bulb-housing of the lamp, the thumb of the other hand hitched securely to my belt to ease the weight of the battery on it. My torch picks out the ties, the rails, the sudden holes and bumps in the rock floor. I curse having refused Bolton's offer of a rope belt on the surface. The surface. It does not exist. It never did. I feel grim and tired, my mind clicking into a dreary, monotonous but not unrestful bitterness, what I taught myself to do after the first five miles of an infantry speed march. Oblivious.

90 Crashing against the protruding ledges and rock kinks, I feel nothing. Dizzyness comes and goes; I force it away with deep breaths. My feet are on fire, clawed and crushed. Size nine on size ten feet. I curse Bolton's canny maliciousness; there is murder in my heart; I curse my own vanity for allowing myself to play the game Bolton's way. Dinlock's way. I am furious, wholeheartedly delivering myself into a fury that I should be here, shambling so clumsily about in these fetid dungeons of coal, instead of having a coffee in Torino's in London. That any human being should have to make his living wage down in this well-wired, blackly populous hell. It is plain bloody 100 ridiculous. I jerk up my head. Something was said. That was me. "It's plain ridiculous." Did MacLane and Bolton hear me? Where are they anyway? I lift the beam of my torch and play it down the thick-smelling blackish grey roadway.

I have fallen too far back. There is nobody in the tunnel, it is deserted. Hunched over, I run forward to what must be a turning. But no, it keeps going on, smaller and shallower, my feet kicking up small fluorescent fluffs of dry coal dust flat yellow in the cloud of my lamp. The car tracks end. Now it is just dust and rock and coal on all sides. I see and hear nothing.

110   I kneel down and my eyes follow the pencil of light. No. Nobody here. Slowly, careful not to let certain thoughts intrude, I kneel around and flash the beam back of me. Nobody there either. I am alone. I drop down on my haunches. I swish my hand on the carpet of coal dust. All of a sudden, I do not dislike being down here by myself.

After a few moments I hear some noises, and I pick myself up and make my way back. At the junction MacLane is patiently waiting. "It's not always a good idea to go off on your own, sir," he says politely. I apologise. We go on.

120   The tunnelled roadway grows progressively more shallow and cramped. The going is tougher because squarely down the middle, raised up to about the level of our bent heads, on a series of metal struts, is a moving conveyor belt, V-shaped, carrying pieces of coal. The conveyor moves with a clackle and a hiss, and the space we move through is only just wide enough for a man with narrow shoulders. The conveyor stops. Another seated fat man in underwear says to MacLane that it has been stopping and starting since the beginning of the shift. Mac-Lane reaches into a cleft in the rock and pulls out a field tele-

130   phone, winds it up and speaks to someone, asking what the trouble is. He nods a few times and replaces the phone. He is concerned but still has time for his guest, pointing out in the same cleft a small locked metal case. He opens it to show me syringes of morphine. "A great help, that," he says. Are there many accidents requiring morphine? "Enough," he says. I remember that on the surface I have often heard the men talk about rock slides in this seam. Later, Davie tells me that Mac-Lane himself, many years ago, was caught in one slide accident which put him in the hospital for six months and left him

140   with a permanently crooked leg.

The conveyor belt starts moving again and so do we. From time to time, as we scramble along, MacLane reaches over and takes a piece of coal off the conveyor belt to examine it. Bolton sees this and says firmly, "Damn' good coal that." MacLane nods coolly.

We continue to encounter small gangs of black men, black all over them, coal dust on every inch of them including the

eye-lids, making the whites of their eyes seem protruding and disembodied. We pass the mouths of other roadways, and I
150 can see tiny points of moving light at the far ends of them. "Face men," says Bolton.

CLANCY SIGAL
Weekend in Dinlock

A. Comprehension and Deduction

1 What problems does the writer encounter when he begins to move down this lower tunnelway?

2 How does he adjust himself to these problems?

3 What are the main bodily discomforts experienced in moving along this tunnelway?

4 In what ways is it obvious that Bolton and MacLane have plenty of experience of these conditions whilst the writer has none?

5 Comment on the ways in which the atmosphere and the appearance of the men encountered change as they move along the tunnel.

6 How does the writer manage to move along the lowest parts of the tunnel?

7 What improvement has been made in the journey from the pit shaft to the coal face since Bolton first worked down this pit?

8 (*a*) What feelings does the writer find himself now possessing which he had previously possessed on infantry marches? (*b*) What is there in common between the two situations?

9 Try to state the main reasons for the writer working himself up into a fury whilst moving along the tunnel.

10 What makes the final stretch of tunnel leading to the face particularly difficult and dangerous to move along?

11 For what purpose does MacLane use the field telephone whilst they are down there?

12 What seems to be the particular natural danger involved in working in this part of the pit?

13 What is the purpose of the morphine syringe and why is MacLane appreciative of this?

14 What is the purpose of the conveyor belt?

15 What are "face-men"?

B. Interpretation and Criticism

1 What is a "seam", as used in this context? (line 8)

2 What is the meaning of "discernible" in the context "but can detect no discernible style"? (line 11)

3 The writer, an American, refers to "the wooden ties of the narrow-gauge tracks". (line 13) By which word would we refer to "ties"?

4 What is a "narrow-gauge" as opposed to a "standard-gauge" track?

5 What appears to be the purpose of the "paddy-train"? (line 23)

6 What is the meaning of the word "conductors" (line 32) as it is used by the writer to describe MacLane and Bolton?

7 "MacLane briefs me." (line 34) What is the meaning of "briefs" in this context?

8 What is the meaning and implication of the word "en-crusted" in the reference to Frank's "grime-encrusted canvas shorts"? (line 44)

9 Why does the writer feel that he may be moving towards "some sort of molten core"? (line 60)

10 Why does the fact that Eddie "isn't a face worker" make it easier to recognise him?

11 What does the word "pendulously" mean and why is it an appropriate word to use in connection with a paunch? (line 73)

12 What is a "canny maliciousness"? (line 92) What differ-ence does the word "canny" make here?

13 Why does the writer use the metaphor "carpet" when he refers to swishing his hand "on the carpet of coal dust"? (line 107)

14 What is a field telephone as opposed to a normal telephone?
15 What is the meaning of the word "disembodied" in the writer's observation, "the whites of their eyes seem protruding and disembodied"? (lines 148-149)

C. Comment and Discussion

The author of this passage, Clancy Sigal, is an American. The passage is taken from a book recording the author's observations and impressions of the coal mining districts of Yorkshire.

1 Compare this passage with Priestley's description of the Goose Fair (No. 4, page 16). Both are written in the first person and both give a subjective impression of what they see and hear.

2 Consider in this passage the ways in which writing in the first person and writing subjectively with plenty of personal expression of reactions and opinions help to make the passage more interesting to read than an impersonal account, written text-book fashion, of a journey to the coal face.

3 What are the advantages of Sigal's approach in books written with a definite informative intention?

4 Consider here the dangers of a subjective approach in a text-book of modern social history. What does the reader have to allow for here?

5 Finally, how does the style of this passage add to one's enjoyment of it and also how does it help to convey effectively the real atmosphere of the coal mine?

Notes on Authors

ALLINGHAM – Margery

The passage entitled "The Kidnappers" has been taken from Margery Allingham's novel *The Tiger in the Smoke*. The action of this story is set in a London fog, and many of its thrilling events revolve around a London street band, typical of the jazz bands, often made up of ex-service men, who play at the kerbside on some of the main shopping streets. The story was made into a highly successful film in the 1950s, and as a result the London street band employed, "The Happy Wanderers", made television appearances and recordings. Just as Conan Doyle created Sherlock Holmes, so Margery Allingham created for her thrillers detective Albert Campion; he appears in *The Tiger in the Smoke*.

ATTENBOROUGH – David

David Attenborough is perhaps best known to the public for his television series of films made on expeditions to such diverse places as Sierra Leone, British Guiana, Indonesia, New Guinea, Paraguay, and Madagascar. These expeditions have also had a zoological purpose: David Attenborough has been searching for rare creatures to bring back and to study. These adventures have been described in his entertaining series of "Zoo Quest" books, the passage "Beasts in the Bathroom" being taken from *Zoo Quest in Paraguay*.

CHANDLER – Raymond

Viewers of B.B.C. television may remember a series of short American thrillers which featured a hard-boiled private detective, Marlowe, a man of few words, who nearly always took heavy beatings before getting his man and who tended to act without the approval of the local D.A. This character was based on the fictional hero of Raymond Chandler's thrillers. Most of these thrillers are set in California, where Raymond Chandler used to live. *The Big Sleep* is written in the first person of Marlowe himself and the tense, grimly humorous style suits the material.

GREY – Zane

Today the Western story is as popular as ever and nowhere more popular than on television where two or three series are always available each week. Before the days of cinema and television a similar taste was for Western novels and few who collected them would be without a Zane Grey Western. Grey was a dentist until a visit to the American West inspired him to write *The Last of the Plainsmen*. This was tremendously popular; other novels, such as *Riders of the Purple Sage*, followed. He was one of the pioneers of the Western novel and set the fashion for many future writers.

GUARDIAN – The

The Guardian newspaper was originally known as *The Manchester Guardian* and, though acknowledged as being one of the big national daily papers, it was published in Manchester and not London. It still keeps its regional flavour in many ways; one of its most famous writers, Neville Cardus, a Mancunian by birth, was for a long time both Music Critic and Cricket Commentator, a suitable combination in a City which is the home of the Hallé Orchestra and which sees many cricketing battles at its well-known ground, Old Trafford.

HOGGART – Richard

Richard Hoggart's own boyhood in a working-class area of the Yorkshire city of Leeds was no doubt in his mind as he wrote the passage entitled, here, " Memories ", which is taken from his book *The Uses of Literacy*. Despite its title and despite the fact that it is actually a sociological study, this book is most lively and readable. It is a detailed study of the effect of popular entertainment, magazines, novels, songs, and social attitudes on working-class life today. The writer is now Professor of English at Birmingham University.

HOLLOWOOD – Bernard

The passage " Making Geography Live " is taken from a collection of Bernard Hollowood's humorous articles and cartoons entitled " Scowle and Other Papers ". Scowle is an imaginary village in the North Midlands; Bernard Hollowood is a native of North Staffordshire. " Making Geography Live " is one of a group of articles dealing with the trials and tribulations of the staff at a school called " St. Morbid's ". Bernard Hollowood has been a regular contributor to *Punch* since 1942 and has been its editor since 1958.

INNES – Hammond

Hammond Innes is a writer of adventure stories set in unusual parts of the world. He has made extensive journeys in search of material for his stories and has given a description of these journeys in a travel book, *Harvest of Journeys*, from which the passage " The Iron Ore Railway " is taken. The visits to Labrador described in this book form the basis of his novel *The Land God Gave to Cain*. Three of his novels, *The Wreck of the Mary Deare*, *Campbell's Kingdom* and *The White South*, have been filmed.

LAWRENCE – D. H.

D. H. Lawrence, son of a miner, spent his childhood at Eastwood near Nottingham. His early life there is recalled extensively in his novel *Sons and Lovers*. Later, after a short period as a teacher, he travelled extensively. *Mercury* was inspired by his travels in South Germany and the Alps, whilst some of his finest writing is to be found in his books about Italy and Mexico, *Etruscan Places* and *Mornings in Mexico*. In New Mexico he lived on a ranch. Although perhaps most known for his novels, Lawrence was also a fine short-story writer, essayist, and poet.

PRIESTLEY – J. B.

English Journey from which the passage "The Goose Fair" is taken describes J. B. Priestley's sad journey through industrial England during the unemployment of the 1930s. The descriptions of his visits to the Potteries, the Black Country, and Liverpool are particularly worth reading; these include passages of comic relief such as his description of a whist drive in Birmingham and his attempts at pottery at the Wedgwood factory. J. B. Priestley is a novelist and playwright as well as being an essayist. His best known novel is *The Good Companions*, the story of a Concert Party, which gives a picture of life "on tour" to small-town music halls now long since closed down.

SANSOM – William

William Sansom is a novelist, and writer of travel books, but has become known mainly through his short stories. These stories often make us experience a single situation as if we were directly involved. We experience in one story the terror of a boy who climbs "the vertical ladder" of a gasometer for a dare, in another the love of a plain girl for a homicidal maniac, in another a ghastly experience of a fireman as he sees a wall toppling on to him and his colleagues. The passage "Fire in a Coffee Warehouse" comes from his story *The Witnesses*, and for its sinister climax the full story should be read.

SILLITOE – Alan

The complete story, *Noah's Ark*, describes two boys' experiences at the Nottingham Goose Fair, and their attempts to gain a free ride on the Noah's Ark roundabout. Alan Sillitoe grew up in working-class Nottingham and worked for a time in a bicycle factory there. His experiences finally inspired the writing of his novel *Saturday Night and Sunday Morning*, which won the Authors' Club Award for the best first novel of 1958 and which was later filmed. One of his finest pieces of writing so far has been his long short story *The Loneliness of the Long Distance Runner*, a study of a Borstal boy's thoughts as he takes part in cross-country running.

SIGAL – Clancy

Coal mines have been the subject of a great deal of sensational writing but if one really wishes to experience the true oppressiveness and real sensation of work at the coal face Clancy Sigal's vivid but matter of fact account of his own visit to a coal face is worth reading. He is a young American writer and *Weekend in Dinlock* is his record of several visits to a number of Yorkshire mining villages in order to find out more about life above and below ground in a typical mining community in the 1960s.

STUCLEY – Elizabeth

Elizabeth Stucley lives in Clapham Common, London, where she founded The Adventurers' Club for the boys and girls of the neighbourhood. Their activities include play-acting, painting and camping. They have been the inspiration for *Magnolia Buildings*, the novel from which the passage

" Ally's New Year Resolution " is taken, and which describes the type of adventures they have, leading up to Ally's last minute success in a school pantomime where she over-acts and enjoys every minute of it.

SUNDAY TELEGRAPH – The

At a time when the closing down of national and regional newspapers was occurring with depressing frequency, a new Sunday paper was announced. Since 1961 *The Sunday Telegraph* has rapidly increased its sales and now seems firmly established. The passage given in this book was a feature article printed as background to the news that Britain's longest non-stop railway journey, until then entrusted to steam locomotive haulage, was to be diesel-hauled.

THOMAS – Dylan

Dylan Thomas spent much of his childhood and youth in and around Swansea and Carmarthen, in South Wales. He remembers these days in his book *Portrait of the Artist as a young Dog*: an Uncle who sang hymns and cursed his mare in Welsh as he drove them home from market, and a Grandpa who, in the dead of night, sat in bed rocking from side to side and shouting " Gee Up! " to imaginary horses. Other memories are present in prose writings such as " Memories of Christmas ", and in many of his poems. Dylan Thomas was predominantly a poet. Several recordings were made of Dylan Thomas reading his own poetry and prose before his tragically early death, and these, as well as revealing his brilliance of voice, emphasise that his highly individual style of writing gains much from being read aloud.

VESEY-FITZGERALD – Brian

Cats, the book from which the passage " The Intelligence of Cats " is taken, claims to be the first complete guide to domestic cats to be published. Its author, Brian Vesey-Fitzgerald, is, like many men, a cat lover, although he has also edited a vast volume of information about every conceivable breed of dog entitled *The Book of the Dog*. He has for many years been an authority on natural history and has been the Editor-in-Chief of *The Field* magazine.

WATERHOUSE – Keith

Like Richard Hoggart, Keith Waterhouse grew up in the city of Leeds. *There is a Happy Land*, his first novel, is a tale of childhood set in a working-class area of Leeds, full of the comedy of youthful gang escapades, fights, and clashes with authority. Finally, a tragedy occurs which no one could really understand. Keith Waterhouse's novel, *Billy Liar*, has been adapted as a successful London play. He has collaborated with Willis Hall on the film script of a fellow Yorkshireman's novel, Stan Barstow's *A Kind of Loving*, and, with Willis Hall, has written a West End revue with a north-country flavour, " England, Our England ".